LET'S HAVE A BRUNCH COOKBOOK

JUNE ROTH'S
LET'S HAVE A BRUNCH
COOKBOOK

AN ESSANDESS SPECIAL EDITION
NEW YORK

LET'S HAVE A BRUNCH COOKBOOK

SBN: 671-10543-4

Published by *Essandess Special Editions*,
a division of Simon & Schuster, Inc.,
630 Fifth Avenue, New York, N.Y. 10020,
and on the same day in Canada
by Simon & Schuster of Canada, Ltd.,
Richmond Hill, Ontario
Printed in the U.S.A.
Designed by Judith C. Allan.

ACKNOWLEDGMENTS

Deep appreciation to the following for their valued information during the preparation of this book:

Accent International, American Molasses Company, California Wine Institute, Campbell Soup Company, Chiffon Margarine Company, Denmark Cheese Association, Descoware Corporation, Diamond Walnut Inc., Duffy-Mott, Inc., Florida Citrus Commission, R.T. French Company, Frito-Lay, Inc., General Foods, Inc., Great Western Champagne & Wine Company, Green Giant Company, Hunt-Wesson Foods, Inc., International Shrimp Council, Kellogg Company, Knox Gelatine, Inc., Louis Sherry, Inc., National Broiler Council, The Nestle Company, Inc., Oscar Mayer & Company, Ocean Spray Cranberries, Inc., Processed Apples Institute, Inc., Rice Council, Seneca Foods Corp., S & W Fine Foods, Seven Seas, Inc., Sunkist Growers, Inc., Swift & Company, McIlhenny Company, Tuna Council, Underwood Company, United Fruit Company, Wasa Company.

To Natalie and Norman,
for warmth and love
that is far beyond the call of duty.

FOREWORD

Dear Reader,

"Let's have a brunch!" is often the ideal solution to problems of entertaining whether celebrating a particular occasion or just feeling convivial.

An American invention, brunch is a clever combination of breakfast and luncheon. It has all the beauty of casual living, catches guests at eye-open hours—anywhere from 11:00 on— and awakens a hostess to a wide range of menu possibilities.

Brunch can be as elegant or as easy as you care to make it. This book has been designed to meet every brunch time need, and includes complete menus and recipes that are both easy to prepare and delicious. Most recipes have been planned to feed eight people, making it a matter of simple mathematics to divide or double quantities in most instances.

The most important requirement of any successful party is a relaxed hostess. Here is a book that will make you just such a hostess. You'll find it easy to entertain and to enjoy your guests when you follow the plans that have been formulated just for the occasion of . . . BRUNCH!

Sincerely,
June Roth

CONTENTS

FOREWORD

Holiday Brunches

NEW YEAR'S DAY BRUNCH 3
ST. VALENTINE'S DAY BRUNCH 9
ST. PATRICK'S DAY BRUNCH 15
EASTER SUNDAY BRUNCH 21
FOURTH OF JULY BRUNCH 25
LABOR DAY BRUNCH 29
HALLOWEEN BRUNCH 33
THANKSGIVING DAY BRUNCH 39
CHRISTMAS DAY BRUNCH 48

Special Occasion Brunches

BIRTHDAY BRUNCH 55
BRIDAL SHOWER BRUNCH 61
WEDDING BRUNCH 67
BABY SHOWER BRUNCH 71
HOUSEWARMING BRUNCH 77
ANNIVERSARY BRUNCH 81
BON VOYAGE BRUNCH 87

WELCOME HOME BRUNCH   *91*
GUEST OF HONOR BRUNCH   *97*
BRIDGE BRUNCH   *103*
BEFORE THE GAME BRUNCH   *109*
GRADUATION BRUNCH   *113*
ENGAGEMENT BRUNCH   *119*
BARBECUE BRUNCH   *125*
APRÈS SKI BRUNCH   *131*

Around the World Brunches

CANADIAN BRUNCH   *139*
CHINESE BRUNCH   *145*
ENGLISH BRUNCH   *149*
FRENCH BRUNCH   *153*
HUNGARIAN BRUNCH   *159*
ISRAELI BRUNCH   *165*
ITALIAN BRUNCH   *171*
MEXICAN BRUNCH   *175*
RUSSIAN BRUNCH   *181*
SCANDINAVIAN BRUNCH   *185*
SPANISH BRUNCH   *189*
VIENNESE BRUNCH   *195*

LET'S HAVE A BRUNCH
COOKBOOK

HOLIDAY
BRUNCHES

*Cream Cheese Scrambled Eggs, Grilled Sausages,
and Cheese 'n' Bacon Nut Loaf.*

NEW YEAR'S DAY BRUNCH

Start the new year surrounded by good friends who want to continue the party mood. The menu is deliberately simple and homey to set any overindulged stomach at rest—yet hearty and satisfying to awakened appetites. Give a warm welcome to another year!

MENU

On arrival:
CRANBERRY CHEER PUNCH*

At the table:
CREAM CHEESE SCRAMBLED EGGS*
GRILLED SAUSAGES*
STUFFED POTATO PANCAKES*
TOASTED ENGLISH MUFFINS
ORANGE MARMALADE

For dessert:
CHEESE 'N' BACON NUT LOAF*
COFFEE

Recipe follows

CRANBERRY CHEER PUNCH

There's plenty of wake-up-and-live spirit in the Cranberry Cheer Punch, enhanced by tiny scoops of lemon sherbet. Have plain orange juice and tomato juice on hand for the guests who want juice straight or with spirits added. Enough variety of libation to please every palate—the morning-after-the-night-before!

1 cup sugar
1 quart cranberry juice
2 cups orange juice
1 cup pineapple juice
¾ cup lemon juice
Ice cubes
2 cups ginger ale
1 pint lemon sherbet

Stir sugar into cranberry juice until dissolved. Pour into punch bowl with other fruit juices. Add a tray of ice cubes. Add ginger ale. Float small scoops of sherbet on top of punch. MAKES 20 ½-CUP SERVINGS.

CREAM CHEESE
SCRAMBLED EGGS

Undercook the Cream Cheese Scrambled Eggs a bit if you plan to serve them in a covered chafing dish over a warmer. Sprinkle chopped chives on the top for extra color and zest, if desired; then surround with piping hot Grilled Sausages—delicious enough to welcome any new day of the year!

2 3-ounce packages cream cheese
½ cup milk
1 dozen eggs
1 teaspoon salt
1 teaspoon Tabasco sauce
4 tablespoons butter

Put cream cheese and milk in a large mixing bowl; blend until smooth. Add eggs, salt, and Tabasco sauce; beat until foamy. Melt butter in a chafing dish or a large skillet; pour in egg mixture. Cook over medium heat, stirring at bottom and sides as eggs become firm. Continue until eggs are thick and creamy.
MAKES 6–8 SERVINGS.

GRILLED SAUSAGES

Place pork sausage links in a cold skillet. Cook over low heat 12–15 minutes, turning often, until browned. Pour off fat as it accumulates.
1 POUND OF SAUSAGE LINKS MAKES 4–6 SERVINGS.

STUFFED POTATO PANCAKES

Here's a quick trick with a convenience food mix. Just what you need to make potato pancakes in a hurry—stirs up fast and browns by the spoonful. Guests will enjoy the surprise filling of deviled ham and cranberry-orange relish. Keep hot on a warming tray, then serve with a dollop of cold sour cream for contrast. Delicious!

2 3-ounce packages potato pancake mix
2 eggs
1 4½-ounce can deviled ham
¼ cup cranberry-orange relish
1 cup sour cream

Continued on next page

STUFFED POTATO PANCAKES/Continued
Prepare potato pancakes according to package directions using 2 eggs. Cook until brown on both sides. Combine deviled ham with cranberry-orange relish. Spread pancakes with deviled ham mixture. Roll and serve hot with sour cream. MAKES 12–14 STUFFED PANCAKES.

CHEESE 'N' BACON NUT LOAF

This Cheese 'n' Bacon Nut Loaf is another recipe that takes advantage of modern products—from the biscuit mix to the shelled walnuts! Make it in advance or serve it warm right from the oven with plenty of hot coffee. While everyone savors the Loaf, make a New Year's resolution to have brunch parties more often!

1 egg
1 cup milk
1 tablespoon instant minced onion
Dash Tabasco sauce
3 cups biscuit mix
¾ cup grated Cheddar cheese
6 strips bacon, cooked crisp and crumbled
¾ cup coarsely chopped walnuts

Beat egg lightly. Add milk, onion, and Tabasco and let stand while measuring remaining ingredients. Stir biscuit mix and cheese together. Add to first mixture, and mix to a stiff dough. Stir in bacon and walnuts. Turn into a greased 9-inch-by-5-inch loaf pan. Bake at 350° for 50 minutes, or until loaf tests done. Let stand 5 minutes, then turn out onto a wire rack to cool. MAKES 1 LOAF.

Open-Hearted Lobster Salad.

ST. VALENTINE'S DAY BRUNCH

Want a heartwarming idea? Invite those you love to a St. Valentine's Day Brunch. Carry out the theme with special paper goods, like red heart-shaped doilies, and use red-colored food wherever possible. Don't worry about saying "I love you"— let the food speak for itself!

MENU

On arrival:
VALENTINE PUNCH*
RED CAVIAR DIP*

At the table:
OPEN-HEARTED LOBSTER SALAD*
MUSHROOM-CHEESE SOUFFLÉ*

For dessert:
RICE BAVARIAN WITH
CHERRY JUBILEE SAUCE*
COFFEE

* *Recipe follows*

VALENTINE PUNCH

*When lemon-lime soda marries cran-
berry juice cocktail, just watch the
sparkle in your guests' eyes. Use tall
thin glasses with plenty of ice cubes—
freeze the cubes with a cherry in each
for extra red decoration!*

1 quart cranberry juice cocktail
2 cups orange juice
1 quart lemon-lime carbonated beverage
Ice cubes frozen with a maraschino
    cherry in each

Combine the cranberry juice and orange juice. Add the lemon-
lime soda just before serving. Pour over ice cubes.
SERVES 10–12.

RED CAVIAR DIP

*Serve plenty of chips and crackers to
dip up the red caviar mixture. Be careful not to mash the tiny red bubbles as
you combine the ingredients. They're a
surprise start to a loving day!*

1 cup dairy sour cream
1 3-ounce package chive cream cheese
¼ teaspoon Worcestershire sauce
4 tablespoons red caviar
Paprika

Mash sour cream and chive cream cheese together until
creamy and well blended. Add Worcestershire sauce. Add red
caviar and mix through. Chill until ready to serve; then transfer to a small bowl and sprinkle paprika over the top. Serve
with chips or crackers.
MAKES ABOUT 1½ CUPS OF DIP.

OPEN-HEARTED LOBSTER SALAD

The red of the lobster nestled into an open-hearted cut tomato is a pretty sight indeed. Serve it with a wedge of Mushroom-Cheese Soufflé that has a quick trick all its own. It's a cupid combination!

4 cups diced cooked or canned lobster
1 cup diced celery
1 cup mayonnaise
¼ cup capers
2 tablespoons lemon juice
1 teaspoon salt
1 teaspoon Tabasco sauce
8 large tomatoes

Combine lobster and celery. Blend together mayonnaise, capers, lemon juice, salt, and Tabasco. Toss ⅔ of this mixture with the lobster. Cut tomatoes in six wedges, cutting almost but not quite through to the bottom, to form the open heart. Place on salad greens and fill center with lobster salad. Serve with remaining mayonnaise mixture.
MAKES 8 SERVINGS.

MUSHROOM-CHEESE SOUFFLE

1 10½-ounce can condensed cream of mushroom soup
1 cup shredded sharp Cheddar cheese
¼ teaspoon chervil
½ cup finely minced cooked ham
2 tablespoons chopped parsley
8 eggs, separated

Continued on next page

MUSHROOM-CHEESE SOUFFLE/Continued

In saucepan, combine soup, cheese, and chervil. Heat slowly until cheese melts, stirring constantly. Remove from heat; add ham and parsley. Beat egg yolks until thick and lemon-colored; gradually stir in soup mixture. Beat egg whites until stiff; fold soup mixture into egg whites. Pour into an ungreased 2-quart casserole. Bake at 300° 1–1¼ hours, or until soufflé is golden brown. Serve immediately.
MAKES 8 SERVINGS.

RICE BAVARIAN

For dessert here's a Rice Bavarian mold that uses convenience foods with gay abandon. Smother it with the rich Cherry Jubilee Sauce and serve with pride. A finale worthy of your loving care!

1⅓ cups packaged precooked rice
1½ cups milk
½ teaspoon salt
1 envelope unflavored gelatin
¼ cup cold water
1 egg, slightly beaten
⅓ cup sugar
¼ teaspoon nutmeg
1 cup milk
1 tablespoon lemon juice
1 envelope whipped topping mix
Cherry Jubilee Sauce (recipe follows)

Combine rice, 1½ cups milk, and the salt in a saucepan. Bring to a full boil, uncovered. Cover; remove from heat. Let stand about 5 minutes, fluffing occasionally with a fork. Meanwhile, soften gelatin in cold water. Combine egg, sugar, nutmeg, 1 cup milk, and the softened gelatin. Add slowly to rice, mixing well. Cook and stir over low heat until mixture coats a metal spoon. Remove from heat. Stir in lemon juice. Chill until slightly thickened. Prepare whipped topping mix as directed on package; fold into rice mixture. Spoon into buttered 5-cup mold. Chill until firm. Unmold and serve with Cherry Jubilee Sauce. MAKES 8 SERVINGS.

Cherry Jubilee Sauce

1 1-pound can pitted, syrup-packed, sweet dark cherries
1 tablespoon cornstarch
Dash of salt
⅓ cup sugar
1 tablespoon butter
2 teaspoons lemon juice

Drain cherries, reserving syrup. Add water to syrup to make 1½ cups. Combine cornstarch, salt, and sugar in a saucepan. Add measured liquid and mix well. Cook and stir over medium heat until mixture comes to a boil. Reduce heat; then continue to cook and stir until sauce is thickened and clear. Remove from heat; add butter and lemon juice. Cool. Add drained cherries to cold sauce. MAKES 3 CUPS.

Walnut-Glazed Corned Beef and Irish Potatoes.

ST. PATRICK'S DAY BRUNCH

Wear the green and serve a new way on St. Patrick's Day—have the bunch in for brunch! Then cook with a green thumb too, and may the luck of the Irish be with you.

MENU

On arrival:
LIMEADE PUNCH*
FISH 'N' DIP

At the table:
WALNUT-GLAZED CORNED BEEF*
IRISH POTATOES*
LIME CABBAGE GELATIN MOLD*

For dessert:
SWEET IRISH SODA BREAD*
MARMALADE
IRISH COFFEE*

Recipe follows

LIMEADE PUNCH

What kind of thirst quencher to greet your guests? Limeade Punch is the perfect color and taste for the day! Add a bit of gin or vodka for those who wish to imbibe, and float thin lime slices for all. A sprig of mint adds a bit of taste and puts all in clover!

1 6-ounce can frozen limeade
1 quart ginger ale
1 fresh lime
Sprigs of mint leaves
Ice cubes

In a large pitcher, mix frozen limeade with water as directed on the package. Add ginger ale just before serving. Add paper-thin slices of fresh lime, and sprigs of mint leaves for garnish. Serve over ice cubes in long-stemmed wine glasses.
MAKES 8 SERVINGS.

FISH 'N' DIP

Simple fried fish is a standard meal in Erin, but here it becomes a tasty appetizer. Dunk it in the zesty green sauce, and get a toothsome morsel every time!

1 pound flounder, haddock, or cod fillets
½ cup flour
½ teaspoon salt
1 cup cooking oil
½ cup tartar sauce
Green food coloring
1 fresh lemon

Cut fish into bite-sized pieces. Combine flour and salt; coat fish pieces with this mixture. Heat cooking oil in a small skillet; fry pieces of fish until golden brown. Remove to paper toweling to absorb excess oil. Mix tartar sauce with several drops of green coloring until it reaches an appropriate Irish-green color. Arrange a platter with a bowl of the tartar sauce mixture in the center and the fish bits all around. Slice a lemon paper thin, and use as a garnish. Serve with hors d'oeuvre picks. MAKES 8 SERVINGS.

WALNUT-GLAZED CORNED BEEF

Instead of boiling corned beef the traditional way, get one specially prepared for oven roasting. Then smother it in a clove-spiced honey and walnut glaze, and serve with buttered parsley potatoes. What a way to make sure that Irish eyes are smiling!

4- to 5-pound corned beef (prepared for oven roasting)
½ cup honey
⅛ teaspoon ground cloves
2 tablespoons chopped walnuts

Roast corned beef in an open pan for 2½–3 hours at 350°; test with a fork for tenderness. In a saucepan, combine honey, ground cloves, and walnuts. Spoon this glaze over the corned beef 10 minutes before serving. MAKES 8–12 SERVINGS.

IRISH POTATOES

2 16-ounce cans whole small potatoes, drained
¼ cup melted butter
2 tablespoons chopped parsley

Place potatoes in a small casserole. Pour melted butter over and coat them well. Sprinkle with parsley. Heat for 10–15 minutes in a 350° oven (along with the corned beef). MAKES 8 SERVINGS.

LIME CABBAGE GELATIN MOLD

Sour cream pales the green of this gelatin mold to a mere tint of the color. But it is emboldened by slices of olives and cobwebs of cabbage, giving tang and crunch to every bite!

1 6-ounce package lime gelatin
2 cups hot water
½ cup cold water
1 cup sour cream
1 cup sliced pimiento-stuffed olives
1 cup thinly shredded green cabbage

Empty gelatin into a bowl; dissolve with hot water. Add cold water, then sour cream; stir well. Add sliced olives and shredded cabbage. Pour into 1½-quart mold and refrigerate until solid. Unmold and serve on a nest of salad greens.
MAKES 8 SERVINGS.

SWEET IRISH SODA BREAD

It wouldn't be a proper celebration without a traditional Irish Soda Bread! Buy it at your local bakery, or get inspired and bake your own—either way, serve it for dessert with orange marmalade.

2 cups all-purpose flour
1½ teaspoons baking powder
¼ teaspoon baking soda
1 teaspoon salt
3 tablespoons sugar
1 tablespoon caraway seeds
½ cup raisins or dried currants
1 cup buttermilk
Orange marmalade

Mix flour, baking powder, baking soda, salt, and sugar together. Add caraway seeds and raisins. Stir in buttermilk to make a soft dough. Knead dough on a lightly floured board for about a minute; then shape it into a round loaf and put it into an 8-inch greased round pan. Pat flour lightly over the top surface, then cut crosswise into the top. Bake in a preheated 350° oven for 40 minutes, or until done. Bread should have a hollow sound when you tap it. For plain bread, omit the caraway seeds and raisins. Serve with orange marmalade.
MAKES 8 SERVINGS.

IRISH COFFEE

Top your brunch off with the best taste treat of all—a tall glass of traditional Irish Coffee. Savor the hot whiskey-coffee mixture as it joins the cold whipped cream. Begorrah . . . it's so good!

1 jigger Irish whiskey
1 teaspoon sugar
6 ounces strong coffee
Chilled sweetened whipped cream
Dash of crème de menthe (optional)

For each serving, pour a jigger of Irish whiskey into a footed glass (or coffee cup if preferred). Add sugar and fill with strong coffee to ½ inch from the top. Cover the top ½ inch with sweetened whipped cream and pour a dash of crème de menthe in the center.
MAKES 1 SERVING.

*Glazed Bacon Roast, Spicy Waffles and
Fluffy Orange and Lemon Toppings.*

EASTER SUNDAY BRUNCH

You can decorate your Easter eggs to your heart's content—then use them as a centerpiece, and finally as part of your brunch menu. One time when creativity has many rewards!

MENU

On arrival:
ORANGE JUICE
CHEDDAR BUNNIES*

At the table:
GLAZED BACON ROAST*
SPICY WAFFLES WITH
FLUFFY ORANGE OR LEMON TOPPING*
HARD-COOKED EASTER EGGS
HOT CROSS BUNS

For dessert:
SHERRY COCONUT CREAM PIE*
COFFEE

* Recipe follows

CHEDDAR BUNNIES

Have a large pitcher of orange juice ready, with spirits nearby for those who wish to add it. Then watch those Cheddar Bunnies do a disappearing act!

1 cup Cheddar cheese spread
¼ cup sesame seeds
Several cherries

With floured hands, roll the cheese into small balls, using about 1½ teaspoons of cheese for each. Roll the balls in the sesame seeds; then pinch up two "ears." Cut the cherries in tiny pieces, and place two "eyes" on each bunny head. Serve on a bed of parsley.

MAKES ABOUT 30 PIECES.

GLAZED BACON ROAST

You'll get more compliments for this Glazed Bacon Roast than for your Easter bonnet!

½ cup whole cranberry sauce
¼ cup prepared yellow mustard
2 tablespoons honey
Whole Canadian bacon, approximately
    2 pounds

Combine cranberry sauce, mustard, and honey; spread generously over Canadian bacon. Roast in 350° oven gauging 25 minutes per pound, spooning glaze over meat frequently during roasting.

MAKES 8 SERVINGS.

SPICY WAFFLES

These Spicy Waffles have two kinds of fluffy toppings—a difficult choice as both are luscious.

3 cups sifted all-purpose flour
2 teaspoons baking powder
2 tablespoons sugar
1 teaspoon salt
1 teaspoon cinnamon
¼ teaspoon allspice
¼ teaspoon nutmeg
6 eggs, separated
2 cups milk
½ cup melted butter
Fluffy Orange Topping (recipe follows)
Fluffy Lemon Topping (recipe follows)

Sift together flour, baking powder, sugar, salt, and spices. Beat egg whites until stiff peaks form. Blend egg yolks, milk, and melted butter; stir into flour mixture. Fold in beaten egg whites. Bake in a preheated waffle iron. Serve with orange and lemon toppings.
MAKES 8 WAFFLES.

Fluffy Orange Topping

Beat together 1 8-ounce package softened cream cheese, ¼ cup confectioner's sugar, and 1 teaspoon grated orange peel until light and fluffy.

Fluffy Lemon Topping

Beat together ½ cup soft butter, 1 tablespoon honey, and 1 teaspoon grated lemon peel until light and fluffy.

SHERRY COCONUT CREAM PIE

A dessert to remember tops off your Easter Brunch—prebake your pie crust whether you make it yourself or buy it frozen. It's the filling that merits your attention!

⅔ cup sugar
½ cup cornstarch
½ teaspoon salt
2½ cups milk
3 egg yolks
½ cup sherry
1 teaspoon vanilla
1 3½-ounce can flaked coconut
1 9-inch baked pie shell
1 cup whipping cream
1 tablespoon sugar

Stir sugar, cornstarch, and salt together until blended. Heat milk. Slowly stir in dry ingredients. Cook and stir over moderate heat until filling boils and thickens, 5–10 minutes. Beat egg yolks; blend with sherry. Add to hot filling and cook 2–3 minutes longer. Remove from heat; add vanilla. Beat filling with rotary beater until smooth and fluffy. Stir in all but ½ cup coconut. Cover pan and cool, then turn filling into baked pie shell. Chill until firm. Beat cream and 1 tablespoon sugar together to moderately stiff peaks. Spread over top of pie; sprinkle with remaining coconut. Refrigerate until ready to serve.

MAKES 8 SERVINGS.

FOURTH OF JULY BRUNCH

Start celebrating your independence with a friendly brunch. Here's a menu that copes with the heat of the day by providing plenty of cool relief!

MENU

On arrival:
BLOODY MARY*
SALAMI FIRECRACKERS*

At the table:
HOT CORN FRITTERS WITH SAUSAGES*
SPICED APPLE RINGS
ASPARAGUS TIPS
TOAST

For dessert:
HONEY CRUNCH SUNDAE PIE*
COFFEE

Recipe follows

BLOODY MARY

Serve plain tomato juice on the rocks to those guests who prefer it—and pass the Salami Firecrackers to all. You'll light a fire under every appetite!

6 ounces tomato juice
2 ounces vodka
Dash of Tabasco sauce
1 teaspoon Worcestershire sauce
Juice of a lemon wedge
Ice cubes

Stir the tomato juice and vodka together in a tall glass. Add Tabasco and squeeze the lemon wedge. Stir and add ice cubes. MAKES 1 DRINK.

SALAMI FIRECRACKERS

1 tablespoon prepared mustard
24 thin slices salami
4 slices processed American cheese

Spread a thin coat of mustard over each slice of salami. Cut each cheese slice into six strips and place 1 strip on each salami slice, overhanging on 1 side. Roll salami up tightly so the protruding strip of cheese looks like the firecracker wick; fasten with a pick. MAKES 24 PIECES.

HOT CORN FRITTERS
WITH SAUSAGES

There'll be a quick parade to the table when your guests get a whiff of these fritters frying! Serve red spiced apple rings for color and flavor contrast—sparks up the taste buds, too.

6 eggs, separated
3 cups cooked kernel corn (may be canned)
1½ teaspoons salt
1 teaspoon Tabasco sauce
½ cup flour
½ cup butter or salad oil
16 sausages

Beat egg yolks until light. Mix in corn, salt, Tabasco sauce, and flour. Beat egg whites until stiff but not dry; fold into corn mixture. Drop by tablespoonsful into hot fat in a skillet. Cook fritters until brown on both sides.

Meanwhile, cook sausages in another skillet, turning until done on all sides. Place in the center of a platter and surround with corn fritters.

MAKES 8 SERVINGS.

HONEY CRUNCH SUNDAE PIE

What could be a better crust for a brunch pie than breakfast cereal itself! Here it is combined with coconut and filled with ice cream—then served with a Creamy Fudge Sauce. Stick a tiny American flag in the center to get into the spirit of the day.

Continued on next page

HONEY CRUNCH SUNDAE PIE/Continued
1½ cups sugar-coated crisp rice cereal
¼ cup honey
2 tablespoons sugar
¼ teaspoon salt
1 tablespoon butter
½ cup flaked coconut, toasted
1 quart vanilla ice cream
Creamy Fudge Sauce (recipe follows)

Place cereal in a greased bowl and set aside. Combine honey, sugar, and salt in a saucepan. Bring to a boil over medium heat, stirring until sugar is dissolved. Continue boiling until a small amount of syrup forms a firm ball in cold water (or to a temperature of 246°). Stir in butter until melted; pour over cereal in bowl, stirring lightly to coat. Add toasted coconut, combine quickly. Press mixture gently on bottom and sides of well-greased 9-inch pie pan. Chill. Fill with vanilla ice cream and serve with Creamy Fudge Sauce.
MAKES 8 SERVINGS.

Creamy Fudge Sauce

3 squares unsweetened chocolate
½ cup light cream
¾ cup sugar
3 tablespoons butter
Dash of salt
¾ teaspoon vanilla

Place chocolate and cream in a saucepan. Stir constantly over low heat until chocolate is melted and mixture is smooth and blended. Add sugar, butter, and salt; continue cooking, stirring constantly, 3–5 minutes longer, or until slightly thickened. Remove from heat and add vanilla. Serve warm or cool.

Note: Store, covered, in refrigerator. Before serving, place bowl of sauce in hot water and stir until smooth.
MAKES 1⅓ CUPS SAUCE.

LABOR DAY BRUNCH

Almost everyone is home on this Monday—so it's a perfect time for a Labor Day Brunch. There's plenty of workmen's compensation in this menu that serves basic food in bouncy new ways!

MENU

On arrival:
APRICOT COOLER*
SAUCY CHICKEN LIVERS*

At the table:
CORNBREAD-SAUSAGE PUFF*
MAPLE SYRUP
ORANGE SLICES WITH MINT

For dessert:
LEMON SHERBET
BUTTERFLY APPLESAUCE CUPCAKES*
COFFEE

* Recipe follows

APRICOT COOLER

Start with a take-it-easy Apricot Cooler that combines juices and carbonated beverage with a soothing touch.

1 quart orange juice
3 cups canned apricot nectar
1 quart lemon-lime carbonated beverage
Ice cubes

Combine orange juice and apricot nectar. Just before serving, stir in carbonated beverage. Add ice cubes.
MAKES 12 SERVINGS.

SAUCY CHICKEN LIVERS

Offer Saucy Chicken Livers from a keep-it-hot chafing dish and let your guests ladle their own over toast triangles. One way of planning less work into the menu!

¼ cup butter
1 pound chicken livers, quartered
¼ pound mushrooms, sliced
¼ cup sliced celery
1 10½-ounce can chicken giblet gravy
Toast triangles

Melt butter in skillet. Brown livers and cook mushrooms and celery until tender. Add gravy. Heat; stir now and then. Pour into heated chafing dish. Serve with toast triangles.
MAKES 8 SERVINGS AS AN APPETIZER; 4 SERVINGS AS A MAIN COURSE.

CORNBREAD-SAUSAGE PUFF

There's a way to put your eggs, bread, and sausage into one dish and to present your guests with a conversation piece: serve this Cornbread-Sausage Puff! Minted orange slices are a perfect side-dish complement for this all-in-one treat.

2 8½-ounce packages cornbread mix
10 eggs
1 pound brown-and-serve sausage links
Butter and maple syrup (optional)

Follow directions on packages for preparing cornbread batter. Put ¼ cup of batter into 10 greased au gratin or individual baking dishes. Drop an egg into the center of the batter in each dish. Place 2 sausages on batter on each side of the egg. (If preferred, arrange ingredients in a large flat casserole pan.) Bake in a moderate oven (375°) for 18–20 minutes, or until eggs are set. Serve with butter and maple syrup, if desired. MAKES 10 SERVINGS.

BUTTERFLY APPLESAUCE CUPCAKES

A serving of lemon sherbet hits the spot at this time, accompanied by fresh-baked cupcakes. A perfect interlude in a day of leisure!

½ cup butter
1 cup firmly packed light brown sugar
2 eggs
1½ cups applesauce
2 cups all-purpose flour
2 teaspoons baking soda
½ teaspoon salt
1 teaspoon ground cinnamon
½ teaspoon ground nutmeg
½ cup chopped nuts
Confectioner's sugar

Cream butter until light and fluffy. Stir in brown sugar and eggs. Beat in 1¼ cups of the applesauce. Sift flour with baking soda, salt, and spices. Stir in flour mixture and nuts. Spoon batter into greased muffin pans, filling each cup ¾ full. Bake in a preheated 350° oven for 20-25 minutes, or until cupcakes spring back when lightly touched. Cool for 5 minutes, then remove cupcakes from pan and cool on a rack. Slice tops from cupcakes. Spoon 1 teaspoon or remaining applesauce over cut surface of each cupcake. Sprinkle each piece sliced from cupcake with confectioner's sugar and cut each in half. Reverse halves and place on top of each cupcake, back to back, to form butterfly wings.
MAKES 12 LARGE CUPCAKES.

HALLOWEEN BRUNCH

Here's a Halloween Brunch that is "gobblin" good! It's full of tricks and treats that will soothe the palates of the witchiest friends you know. Expect all broomsticks to be parked overtime!

MENU

On arrival:
HOT SPICED APPLE NOGGIN*
DEVILISH DANISH*

At the table:
HARVEST SHRIMP CASSEROLE*
RICE RING*
WALDORF WHIP SALAD MOLD*

For dessert:
SHERRY-PUMPKIN CHIFFON PIE*
COFFEE

* Recipe follows

HOT SPICED APPLE NOGGIN

*No need for a cauldron to stir this brew
—but be sure to serve it hot. Not a ghost
of a chance that any will be left over!*

½ cup brown sugar
¼ teaspoon salt
2 sticks whole cinnamon
1 tablespoon whole cloves
¼ teaspoon whole allspice
1 cup water
1 lemon
1 orange
2 quarts apple juice

Combine brown sugar, salt, spices and water; bring to boil.
Reduce heat and simmer 10 minutes. Cut lemon and orange
into thin slices. In a separate saucepan, combine lemon and
orange slices and apple juice. Bring to a boil. Strain hot spiced
liquid into hot apple juice.
MAKES 8 CUPS.

DEVILISH DANISH

*What's so devilish about this Danish?
The use of refrigerator crescent rolls
for the pastry—assemble it in minutes
and bake. All's fair with convenience
foods if the taste pleases!*

1 package refrigerator crescent rolls
1 4½-ounce can deviled ham
½ cup raisins
¼ cup cream or milk

Unroll crescent rolls and separate; cut each triangle in half.
Combine deviled ham and raisins. Place a heaping teaspoon
of the mixture on ½ of each triangle. Flip the other half over

and seal the edges of the dough. Place on a cookie sheet, brush cream over the tops, and bake in a 350° oven for 15 minutes, or until golden brown. Serve hot.
MAKES 20 APPETIZERS.

HARVEST SHRIMP CASSEROLE

Ladle this Harvest Shrimp Casserole over fluffy white rice for a bountiful serving from land and sea. Watch every face light up with a jack-o'-lantern grin!

5 medium green peppers
5 large tomatoes
1 medium eggplant
2 large sweet onions
1½ tablespoons lemon juice
5 small zucchini
4 cloves of garlic
½ cup olive oil
2½ pounds fresh or frozen shrimp, peeled and deveined
1 tablespoon salt
½ teaspoon freshly ground pepper

Clean, peel, and slice the green pepper, tomato, eggplant, and onion. Separate onion into rings. Sprinkle eggplant slices with lemon juice. Remove ends from zucchini and slice thin. Peel and shred garlic cloves and add to olive oil in measuring cup.

In a 4-quart top-of-stove casserole, make layers of onion, green pepper, eggplant, zucchini, tomatoes, and shrimp (in that order). Sprinkle each layer with salt, pepper, olive oil, and garlic, taking care to reserve enough oil for the top layer. Bring to a boil on top of the range; vegetables will form their own cooking liquid almost immediately. Reduce heat to simmer; cover and cook for 30 minutes. To reduce sauce, remove cover and cook 10–20 minutes more.
MAKES 8–10 SERVINGS.

RICE RING

1½ cups instant rice
½ cup chopped pimiento
½ cup chopped parsley

Cook rice according to directions on the package. Fluff it up with a fork. Stir in chopped pimiento and parsley. Pack hot rice into a buttered ring mold. Turn out at once onto a hot platter.
MAKES 8–10 SERVINGS.

WALDORF WHIP SALAD MOLD

A clever sleight-of-hand turns an ordinary Waldorf salad into a creamy luscious offering. What a nutty thing to serve on Halloween!

1 3-ounce package lemon flavored
    gelatin
1 cup hot water
3 tablespoons lemon juice
½ cup mayonnaise
1 cup chopped celery
½ cup chopped walnuts
1½ cups chopped apples
⅔ cup undiluted evaporated milk
Walnut halves
Apple slices

Dissolve gelatin in hot water; cool. Add 1 tablespoon lemon juice, mayonnaise, celery, walnuts, and apples. Mix well. Chill until mixture is the consistency of unbeaten egg whites. Chill evaporated milk in refrigerator ice-cube tray until soft ice crystals form around edges (10–15 minutes). Whip until stiff (1 minute). Add the remaining lemon juice; whip until very

stiff (1–2 minutes longer). Fold whipped evaporated milk into gelatin mixture. Spoon into 5-cup mold. Chill until set (about 2 hours). Unmold on salad greens and garnish with walnuts and raw apple slices.
MAKES 8 SERVINGS.

SHERRY-PUMPKIN CHIFFON PIE

There's nothing pumpkin-headed about this froth of a pie that combines spices and sherry into a conversation piece. Sheer delight in every bite!

3 eggs, separated
½ cup sugar
1 cup canned pumpkin
½ cup light cream
1 teaspoon cinnamon
½ teaspoon nutmeg
⅛ teaspoon ginger
½ teaspoon salt
1 envelope plain gelatin
½ cup sweet sherry
2 tablespoons butter
1 teaspoon vanilla
1 baked, cooled pastry shell*
Whipped cream (optional)

Beat egg yolks until lemony, then beat in sugar. Combine with pumpkin, cream, cinnamon, nutmeg, ginger, and salt. Cook over very low heat, stirring constantly, until mixture thickens. Soften gelatin in sherry; stir into hot pumpkin mixture. Blend in butter and vanilla. Then chill until mixture thickens. Beat egg whites until stiff but not dry. Fold into pumpkin mixture. Mound into baked pastry shell; chill until firm. Garnish or serve with whipped cream, if desired.
MAKES 8 SERVINGS.

* Bake pastry shell in a 10-inch-by-1-inch tart pan or a 9-inch pie pan.

Molasses Pecan Pie.

THANKSGIVING DAY BRUNCH

Although a traditional Thanksgiving celebration is usually held later in the day, there are times when you would rather make it for brunch—because it's an easier meal to serve or because the earlier hour suits you better. Whatever your reason, here's a menu that needs no excuses—it shows evidence of a land of plenty!

MENU

On arrival:
CRANBERRY WHIRL*
ASSORTED CHEESE TRAY

At the table:
BACON-OYSTER CHOWDER*
WAFFLES WITH
HAM AND FRUIT SAUCE*
CRANBERRY-VEGETABLE ASPIC MOLD*
ORANGE-GLAZED TURKEY ROLL*

For dessert:
MOLASSES PECAN PIE*
COFFEE

Recipe follows

CRANBERRY WHIRL

Greet your guests with a frothy glass of Cranberry Whirl and a tray of help-yourself cheeses with assorted crackers. The all-American berry—cranberry— makes a juice that has a special zing to start a special all-American day!

1 quart cranberry juice cocktail
3 pints lemon sherbet

Beat or blend cranberry juice and 2 pints of lemon sherbet until smooth. Pour mixture into tall glasses. Top with scoops of remaining pint of sherbet. Serve with cocktail straws for easier sipping!
MAKES 8 SERVINGS.

BACON-OYSTER CHOWDER

Most of the preparations for Bacon-Oyster Chowder can be made ahead of time, adding milk and oysters just before serving. Do ladle it from a pretty tureen if you can—and hear your guests give thanks that you know how to cook!

½ pound lean bacon, cut into 1-inch
  pieces
1 medium potato, pared and cut in
  ½-inch cubes
1 medium onion, peeled and chopped
1 medium carrot, pared and finely
  chopped
½ cup chopped celery
1 tablespoon chopped green pepper
1½ teaspoons salt
¼ teaspoon pepper
½ cup water
1 quart milk
1 16-ounce can oysters, including liquid

Fry bacon in large heavy kettle until cooked but not crisp. Add vegetables, salt, pepper, and water. Cover and simmer 15–20 minutes. Add milk and bring to simmering point. Add oysters with oyster liquid. Heat only until the edges of oysters curl, about 5 minutes. Serve at once.

MAKES 1½ QUARTS, OR 8 ¾-CUP SERVINGS.

WAFFLES WITH HAM AND FRUIT SAUCE

Take advantage of the bounty of apples at this season, and prepare a sauce for waffles that is lip-smackin' good. Diced ham and raisins make it an unexpected meal in itself.

2 tablespoons butter
¼ cup chopped onion
2 cups canned applesauce
¼ teaspoon ground cloves
⅓ cup seedless raisins
1½ cups diced cooked ham
8 waffles

Melt butter in a skillet and sauté onion until light brown. Add applesauce, cloves, and raisins; simmer 3 minutes. Add ham and heat thoroughly.

Heat frozen waffles, or prepare waffles from a mix, if you wish. Serve hot, with sauce poured over.

MAKES 8 SERVINGS.

CRANBERRY-VEGETABLE ASPIC MOLD

Here's a mini-Thanksgiving Day dinner shimmering on a brunch platter. A cranberry mold of garden vegetables, surrounded by a ring of turkey slices— who could pray for more?

2 envelopes unflavored gelatin
1 pint cranberry juice cocktail
1½ cups apple juice
2 tablespoons lemon juice
1 small onion
1 cup peas, cooked and drained
1 cup sliced carrots, cooked and drained
1 cup sliced raw celery
Slices of orange-glazed turkey roll

In a small saucepan, sprinkle gelatin over ½ cup cranberry juice. Let stand 5 minutes to soften, then heat over low heat, stirring constantly, until gelatin is dissolved. Pour gelatin mixture into remaining cranberry juice; add apple juice and lemon juice. Blend well. Chill until mixture is the consistency of unbeaten egg whites. Fold in vegetables. Pour mixture into a lightly oiled 2-quart mold. Chill until firm and unmold on salad greens. Surround with turkey slices.
MAKES 8 SERVINGS.

ORANGE-GLAZED TURKEY ROLL

1 boned turkey roll (5–7 pounds)
½ cup orange marmalade
2 tablespoons butter

Arrange turkey roll in a small roasting pan. In a saucepan, heat marmalade and butter until they are blended, stirring constantly. Paint turkey roll with half this glaze and roast in a 350° oven for 2½–3 hours. Paint with remaining glaze

several times during roasting. Remove roast from oven and let it "rest" for at least 20 minutes before slicing—it will slice easier.
MAKES 8–10 SERVINGS.

MOLASSES PECAN PIE

The base for this pecan pie is that grand old American sweetener—molasses. One bite will set every sweet tooth atingle and wishing for more! Better double the recipe and make a second one for reserve.

3 eggs, slightly beaten
¾ cup unsulphured molasses
¾ cup light corn syrup
2 tablespoons melted butter
⅛ teaspoon salt
1 teaspoon vanilla
1 tablespoon flour
1 cup pecan pieces
1 8-inch unbaked pastry shell

Combine eggs, molasses, corn syrup, melted butter, salt, and vanilla in a mixing bowl. Make a paste of small amount of the mixture and flour; stir into the remaining mixture. Add the pecans. Turn into unbaked pastry shell. (Use frozen pie shell if you wish.) Bake in a 325° oven for 1 hour, or until firm.
MAKES 8 SERVINGS.

Steamed Snowball Pudding.

CHRISTMAS DAY BRUNCH

Everyone's anxious to open the presents, so start the festivities early with a Christmas Day Brunch. Here's an elegant menu that can be prepared in advance and yet served with pride. It will please good little girls and boys of all ages!

MENU

On arrival:
EGGNOG*

At the table:
CREAMED HAM AND ARTICHOKE HEARTS*
FRUIT SALAD MOLD*
SLICED TURKEY
ASPARAGUS WITH PIMIENTO STRIPS*

For dessert:
STEAMED SNOWBALL PUDDING*
COFFEE

* Recipe follows

EGGNOG

Use commercially prepared eggnog, since it is plentiful at this season—flavor each glass with a sprinkling of grated orange rind and a dash of nutmeg. Or start from scratch and make your own.

4 eggs
2 tablespoons sugar
1 quart milk
1 teaspoon vanilla extract
Grated orange rind
Nutmeg
¼ cup rum, brandy, or whiskey
   (optional)

Beat eggs well. Add sugar, milk, and vanilla; stir until smooth. Add a sprinkling of orange rind and a dash of nutmeg to each serving. If desired, add ¼ cup rum, brandy, or whiskey to the mixture before stirring smooth.
MAKES 8 SERVINGS.

CREAMED HAM
AND ARTICHOKE HEARTS

'Tis the season to be jolly—and here to help you on your way is a novel approach to ham and eggs for breakfast: cut up and casseroled with other goodies. Prepare it a day ahead and refrigerate until the last reindeer hoof is heard. Then bake it hot and serve it bubbly!

2 9-ounce packages frozen artichoke
hearts
1 bay leaf
2 cups diced cooked ham
8 hard-cooked eggs, quartered
2 10½-ounce cans condensed cream of
mushroom soup
¼ cup sherry
1 tablespoon chopped onion
½ teaspoon salt
¼ teaspoon garlic salt
Dash of pepper
4 slices processed American cheese

Cook artichokes as directed on package, adding bay leaf before
simmering. Drain. Discard bay leaf. Arrange artichokes, ham,
and eggs in a 3-quart casserole. Combine soup, sherry, onion,
salt, garlic salt, and pepper; pour mixture into casserole. Top
with cheese. Bake at 400° for 25–30 minutes, or until cheese
is lightly browned.
MAKES 8 SERVINGS.

FRUIT SALAD MOLD

*Santa's belly would shake like jelly if
he could taste this shimmering delight!
Salad dressing and fruit syrup help to
make it extra rich. Take a shortcut and
buy turkey roll slices from your local
delicatessen, or roast your own the day
before, and slice thin.*

Continued on next page

FRUIT SALAD MOLD/Continued
2 envelopes unflavored gelatin
1 cup cold water
1 6-ounce can frozen orange juice
   concentrate, unthawed
1 16-ounce can apricot halves
1 16-ounce can fruit cocktail
1 cup mayonnaise-type salad dressing
1 pound turkey roll, sliced (or cook your
   own if you prefer)

Sprinkle gelatin over water in saucepan. Place over low heat; stir constantly until gelatin dissolves, 3–5 minutes. Remove from heat. Add frozen orange juice concentrate; stir until melted. Drain apricots and fruit cocktail, reserving syrup. Gradually blend syrup into salad dressing; blend into gelatin mixture. Chill until mixture mounds slightly when dropped from spoon. Cut apricot halves in 4 pieces; add to fruit cocktail and fold into gelatin mixture. Turn into oiled 6-cup mold. Chill until firm. Unmold on large platter; arrange turkey slices around the mold, and garnish with salad greens.
MAKES 8 SERVINGS.

ASPARAGUS WITH PIMIENTO STRIPS

Here are red and green bundles that carry out the color scheme while pleasing the palate. All that's missing is a sprig of mistletoe. Do hang some from the chandelier and turn strangers into kissin' cousins!

2 1-pound cans slender green asparagus
    stalks, drained
2 pimientos, cut in long strips

Arrange asparagus on a platter, being careful not to break the tender stalks. Garnish with strips of pimiento.
MAKES 8 SERVINGS.

STEAMED SNOWBALL PUDDING

Invite at least three wise men to taste this steamed pudding. The ingredients are easily available today, but the taste is traditionally old-fashioned. You'll see a wreath of smiles with every serving!

½ cup thinly sliced or chopped candied
    orange peel
½ cup chopped dates, figs, or prunes
1½ cups seedless raisins
½ cup sherry
3 cups sifted all-purpose flour
½ cup sugar
1 teaspoon baking soda
1½ teaspoons salt
1 teaspoon cinnamon
½ teaspoon ginger
½ teaspoon nutmeg
½ teaspoon allspice
1 cup peeled and grated apple
1 cup finely chopped suet
½ cup light molasses
¾ cup milk
Brandied Hard Sauce (recipe follows)

Continued on next page

STEAMED SNOWBALL PUDDING/Continued

Mix orange peel, dates, raisins, and sherry. Cover and let
stand overnight. Resift flour with sugar, baking soda, salt,
and spices into large mixing bowl. Add apple, suet, molasses,
and milk; stir until completely blended. Add sherried fruits
and mix well. Turn into a greased pudding mold (2- to 2½-
quart size) or 2 smaller molds about 1½ quarts each. Cover
molds tightly. Place on rack in a kettle of boiling water. Water
should come halfway up sides of mold. Cover kettle tightly
and steam in continuously boiling water (replenish water as
needed during steaming) about 3 hours for large mold, 2–2½
hours for smaller molds. Remove cover and turn pudding
out on serving dish. Serve with Brandied Hard Sauce rolled
in shredded coconut.
SERVES 10–12.

Brandied Hard Sauce

¼ pound butter
¾ cup confectioner's sugar
2 ounces brandy
1 cup shredded coconut

Cream the butter and sugar together until light and fluffy. Beat in the brandy; smooth into 1-inch balls and roll in shredded coconut. Place on top of pudding, or around the base.

SPECIAL OCCASION BRUNCHES

Chicken 'n' Ham "Birthday Cake."

BIRTHDAY BRUNCH

Start early in the day to celebrate a loved one's birthday. Here's a brunch menu that will appeal to birthday boys and girls—from the tempestuous teens to the sentimental seventies!

MENU

On arrival:
TUTTI-FRUTTI PUNCH*
COCKTAIL FRANKS WITH APRICOT DIP*

At the table:
CHICKEN 'N' HAM "BIRTHDAY CAKE"*
MACARONI AND CHEESE CASSEROLE*
TOSSED SALAD

For dessert:
PEACH SUNBURSTS*
COFFEE, MILK, OR SODA

Recipe follows

TUTTI-FRUTTI PUNCH

Greet each guest with a glass of Tutti-Frutti Punch—with a fruit surprise in every sip.

1 46-ounce can Hawaiian-style fruit
    drink
1 16-ounce can diced fruit cocktail
1 quart ginger ale

Combine fruit drink with diced fruit cocktail, including juice from fruit. Chill. Add chilled ginger ale just before serving to keep it bubbly.

MAKES ABOUT 24 PUNCH-CUP SERVINGS.

COCKTAIL FRANKS WITH APRICOT DIP

Have hot grilled cocktail franks just ready to be dipped in the tangy sauce. Show there's a real party in the air!

24 cocktail franks
1 cup apricot jam
2 tablespoons prepared mustard

Boil or broil franks until done, then spear each one with a pick. Keep warm. Combine apricot jam and mustard in a small bowl. Use as dip for the cocktail franks.

MAKES 8 SERVINGS.

CHICKEN 'N' HAM "BIRTHDAY CAKE"

As long as you're getting a jump on the celebration, why have to wait until dessert for a serving of birthday cake? Here's a switch—a chicken and ham filled "cake" complete with candles for the main course!

Cake

1 8-ounce package cream cheese, at
   room temperature
⅔ cup soft-type margarine
3 cups finely chopped chicken
1 tablespoon lemon juice
1 teaspoon curry powder
¼ teaspoon nutmeg
3 cups finely chopped ham
⅓ cup pickle relish
3 tablespoons prepared mustard
20 slices sandwich bread, crusts
   removed

Blend together cream cheese and margarine. Divide mixture into 2 equal parts. To 1 part add chicken, lemon juice, curry powder, and nutmeg. To second part add ham, pickle relish, and mustard. Place 4 bread slices in a square on a serving platter, spread with half of chicken mixture. Top with 4 more bread slices and half of ham mixture. Repeat, and top with last 4 bread slices. Then frost according to directions below.

Frosting and Decoration

2 8-ounce packages cream cheese, at
   room temperature
½ cup soft-type margarine
½ cup chopped parsley
Green food coloring
Birthday candles
Parsley sprigs

Continued on next page

FROSTING AND DECORATION/Continued

Blend together cream cheese and margarine. Reserve ¾ cup of mixture; spread the rest over outside of cake. Blend together reserved cheese mixture, parsley, and a few drops of green food coloring. To make candle holders, force this mixture through a cake decorator to make rosettes. Insert candles in rosettes. Place parsley sprigs around base of cake.

Note: Cake may be frozen (without parsley and candles). Freeze uncovered just until frosting is hard, then wrap tightly and return immediately to the freezer. For serving, allow to thaw in refrigerator overnight.

MAKES 12 SERVINGS.

MACARONI AND CHEESE CASSEROLE

What makes a superquick sauce for the Macaroni Casserole? Soup! This can be prepared in advance and tucked into the refrigerator, then baked just before serving time. Don't expect leftovers!

1 pound elbow macaroni
1 10½-ounce can condensed cream of
    mushroom soup
4 slices American cheese
3 tablespoons bread crumbs
2 tablespoons butter

Cook macaroni as directed on the package. Drain. Return to saucepan and stir in condensed cream of mushroom soup. Cut up slices of cheese and stir through. Empty this mixture into a greased casserole, sprinkle top with bread crumbs and dots of butter. (Refrigerate until ready to bake.) Bake in a 350° oven for 20 minutes, until hot and bubbly. MAKES 8 SERVINGS.

PEACH SUNBURSTS

A real birthday party has to have ice cream, too. Here's a charming way to serve it. First bake nests of meringue, and then follow directions for Peach Sunbursts. Hope the birthday year to follow will be as yummy good!

4 egg whites
¼ teaspoon salt
1 cup sugar
1 teaspoon almond extract
1 3½-ounce can moist flaked coconut
2 cups sliced peaches
¼ cup sugar
2 teaspoons lemon juice
2 pints vanilla ice cream
5 maraschino cherries, halved

Line baking sheet with brown paper. Add salt to egg whites and beat until frothy. Add sugar gradually, then the almond extract. Beat until mixture is very stiff and forms peaks. With a pastry bag or a spoon, drop meringue on brown paper on baking sheet and shape into 10 shells, 3 inches in diameter. Bottom of shell should be no more than ¼ inch thick and the sides about 1½ inches high. Sprinkle nests with coconut. Bake at 275° about 50 minutes. Remove from paper and place on a cake rack to cool. Sprinkle peaches with sugar and lemon juice. Place a scoop of ice cream in each meringue shell; arrange peach slices on ice cream in sunburst fashion and top with maraschino cherry half. MAKES 10 SERVINGS.

*Chicken Salad Molds, Spiced Peaches,
and Toasted Biscuits.*

BRIDAL SHOWER BRUNCH

Have the girls in for a shower brunch with this cook-ahead menu. Such fun to fete the bride-to-be with things she will need for her own housekeeping days. Do follow the custom and decorate a box-top bonnet with bows from every present!

MENU

On arrival:
PINK LADY COCKTAIL*
BANANA COCONUT BITES*

At the table:
CHICKEN SALAD MOLDS*
SPICED PEACHES*
TUNA AND NOODLE STROGANOFF*
TOASTED BISCUITS*
TOMATO SLICES
RADISHES AND OLIVES

For dessert:
MOCHA WALNUT TORTE*
COFFEE

* Recipe follows

PINK LADY COCKTAIL

While you are all waiting to surprise the bride, pass around a tray of Pink Ladies in tall stemmed glasses. Follow it up with Banana Coconut Bites— garnish with whole strawberries if you can. Can't you almost hear the wedding bells ringing?

1 46-ounce can pineapple juice
2 tablespoons grenadine
Maraschino cherries with stems

Combine pineapple juice with grenadine. Pour into stemmed glasses. Add a cherry to each drink.
MAKES 10–12 SERVINGS.

BANANA COCONUT BITES

3 large ripe bananas
2 drops red food coloring
½ cup dairy sour cream
1 cup shredded coconut

Peel and cut bananas in chunks about 1 inch thick. Stir red food coloring into sour cream, making it a bright pink color. Dip each slice of banana in sour cream and roll in shredded coconut. Chill.
MAKES ABOUT 24 PIECES.

CHICKEN SALAD MOLDS

These individual Chicken Salad Molds are super easy to make. Packaged chicken gravy mix is used for special flavoring. If you don't have time to poach your own chicken for dicing, buy thick slices of cooked chicken roll from your local delicatessen. Color and flavor contrast is provided by the spiced peaches.

2 1¼-ounce envelopes chicken gravy
  mix
2 envelopes unflavored gelatin
3 cups water
4 cups diced cooked chicken
½ cup mayonnaise
1 cup finely diced celery
2 tablespoons diced pimiento
Lettuce leaves
Mayonnaise and chopped pecans
  (optional)

In a saucepan combine the chicken gravy mix and gelatin. Gradually stir in the water. Place over heat and bring to a boil, stirring constantly. Add chicken; cool slightly. Add mayonnaise, celery, and pimiento. Fill 8–12 lightly oiled custard cups or molds. Chill several hours or until firm. Unmold; serve on crisp lettuce leaves. If desired, top with a spoonful of mayonnaise and a few chopped pecans.
MAKES 8–12 SERVINGS.

SPICED PEACHES

2 29-ounce cans peach halves
½ cup water
4 sticks cinnamon
¼ cup lemon juice
½ teaspoon ground cloves
Whole cloves

Drain syrup from peaches into a small saucepan. Add water, cinnamon, lemon juice, and ground cloves. Bring to a boil. Place peaches in a shallow dish; stick 2 or 3 cloves in each half; pour hot syrup over peaches. Chill for several hours or overnight.
MAKES 8–12 SERVINGS.

TUNA AND NOODLE STROGANOFF

Here's a dish that belies its manufactured origins—goes together in minutes and looks like hours of diligent preparation. Just the kind of recipe the bride-to-be will want to have, too!

2 10-ounce cooking pouches frozen
   sweet peas in butter sauce
2 5¾-ounce packages noodles with sour
   cream and cheese sauce mix
1 cup milk
2 7-ounce cans tuna, drained and flaked
½ cup sliced black olives
¼ cup chopped pimiento

Slip pouches of sweet peas into boiling water. Bring water to a second boil; continue cooking 14 minutes. Cook noodles in boiling salted water for 6–7 minutes; drain well. In saucepan, combine noodles, packet of cheese sauce mix, milk, tuna, olives, and pimiento. Heat through.
MAKES 10–12 SERVINGS.

TOASTED BISCUITS

Mustard and butter give these refrigerator biscuits an unusual flavor. Bake them in advance and slip them under the broiler just before serving. You'll have showers of compliments!

1 package refrigerator biscuits
¼ cup soft butter
1 tablespoon prepared mustard
¼ teaspoon celery salt

Bake biscuits as directed on package. Cool. Meanwhile, blend together soft butter and mustard. Add celery salt. Split biscuits; spread tops with mixture. Place on a cookie sheet; broil until lightly toasted. Serve hot.
MAKES 20 TOASTED BISCUITS.

MOCHA WALNUT TORTE

The bride-to-be and all her friends will be sure to rave about this Mocha Walnut Torte. It starts out as a convenience brownie mix and ends up slathered with whipped cream and nuts. Naughty and ever so delicious!

2 eggs
¼ cup water
1 1-pound package plain brownie mix
¾ cup coarsely chopped walnuts
2 cups whipping cream
½ cup firmly packed brown sugar
2 tablespoons instant coffee
Walnut halves

Stir eggs and water into brownie mix, then add chopped walnuts. Spoon into 2 greased 9-inch layer cake pans. Bake at 350° for 20 minutes. Turn out on racks to cool. Whip cream until it begins to thicken; gradually add brown sugar and instant coffee. Continue beating until of spreading consistency. Spread between layers and swirl over top and sides of torte. Polka dot top and sides with walnut halves. Chill overnight.
MAKES 10–12 SERVINGS.

Ham Mousse.

WEDDING BRUNCH

*Planning a wedding brunch at home?
Don't despair—here's a charming menu
that can be prepared ahead of time. Let
your favorite bakery make the wedding
cake. Then let the champagne flip you
into a memorable day!*

MENU

On arrival:
CHAMPAGNE FLIP*
CHEESE-PIMIENTO ROUNDS*

At the table:
HAM MOUSSE*
CHICKEN SHORTCAKE*
ASPARAGUS TIPS

For dessert:
WEDDING CAKE
COFFEE

* Recipe follows

CHAMPAGNE FLIP

Combine champagne and sauterne with a mound of orange sherbet—just the glamor touch you need to get the wedding off to a good march. Serve with cheese rounds boasting bows of brightly colored pimiento. Ask the groom if he likes the taste, and he'll say, "I do."

1 bottle sauterne
2 bottles champagne
1 quart orange sherbet
Ice ring or cubes

Pour chilled wine and champagne over a mound of sherbet in a punch bowl. Add a molded ring of ice, or ice cubes. Scoop up a little sherbet with every serving.
MAKES ABOUT 24 SERVINGS.

CHEESE-PIMIENTO ROUNDS

24 slices white bread
2 3-ounce packages cream cheese
1 8½-ounce can crushed pineapple,
   drained
¼ cup heavy cream
4 whole pimientos

With a round cookie cutter, cut two circles out of each slice of bread. (Use leftover bread for making your own bread crumbs.) Combine cream cheese, crushed pineapple, and cream until light and fluffy. Spread on bread rounds. Slice pimientos crosswise, making 12 circles from each. Place 1 circle on each cheese round, pinching in the center to form a bow. Arrange carefully in shallow pans so they do not overlap. Cover with a wrung-out dampened dishcloth—take care that the cloth does not touch the tops of the cheese rounds.
MAKES 4 DOZEN.

HAM MOUSSE

This richly flavored Ham Mousse is elegant enough to headline the reception party. Make one for every eight guests and garnish with curly greens. Then let your refrigerator keep things cold while you warm up to the wedding day!

1 tablespoon unflavored gelatin
¼ cup cold water
¾ cup boiling water
¼ teaspoon salt
3 tablespoons vinegar
1 tablespoon prepared mustard
1 cup sour cream
½ cup mayonnaise
1 17-ounce can early peas with onions, drained
1 cup finely diced cooked ham
¼ cup finely diced celery

Soften gelatin in cold water in a mixing bowl. Stir in boiling water, salt, and vinegar. Cool slightly. Add prepared mustard, sour cream, and mayonnaise; beat until creamy and smooth. Chill until partially set. Fold in remaining ingredients. Pour into a well-oiled 1½-quart ring mold. Chill several hours or until firm. Unmold on serving plate and garnish with curly greens.
MAKES 8 SERVINGS.

CHICKEN SHORTCAKE

Nothing quite like old-fashioned Chicken Shortcake to give security to a brand new marriage! Split biscuits are smothered with hot saucy chicken—ladled from a chafing dish. Elegant and easy.

To Cook Hen

4- to 6-pound hen (stewing chicken)
3 cups water
1 onion, sliced
2 celery tops
2 bay leaves
2½ teaspoons salt
10 peppercorns

Place chicken in a deep kettle. Add water and remaining ingredients; cover. Bring to boil, then reduce heat and simmer for 2 hours or until tender. Remove chicken; strain broth and reserve. Remove meat from bones; dice meat. Refrigerate diced chicken and broth at once.

To Make Sauce

5 tablespoons flour
2½ cups chicken broth
6 cups diced chicken
1 4-ounce can sliced mushrooms
⅓ cup chopped pimiento
8 large biscuits, bought or homemade

Blend flour with ½ cup of the broth in a saucepan; gradually stir in remaining broth. Place over medium heat and bring to boil, stirring constantly. Cook, stirring, until thickened. Stir in chicken, mushrooms, and pimiento. Heat to serving temperature. To serve, spoon over split biscuits.
MAKES 8 SERVINGS.

BABY SHOWER BRUNCH

When a good friend whispers her baby news to you, plan to celebrate the impending arrival with a Baby Shower Brunch. Here's a menu that will make "eating for two" a pleasure!

MENU

On arrival:
LULLABY PUNCH*
SHERRIED CHEESE MOLD AND CRACKERS*

At the table:
MELON AND GRAPE BOWL
PUFFY SCRAMBLED EGGS*
CHICKEN SUPREME*
SESAME TRIANGLES*

For dessert:
ORANGE PIE*
COFFEE

* Recipe follows

LULLABY PUNCH

This punch is definitely "thinking pink," a pleasant contrast to the wishful-blue bows on many of the baby gifts. Either way, a lovely cupful of warm wishes for a brand new person!

1 46-ounce can pink pineapple-
    grapefruit drink
1 quart raspberry soda
1 pint raspberry sherbet
Ice cubes

Empty pineapple-grapefruit drink into a punch bowl. Just before serving, add raspberry soda and float raspberry sherbet with ice cubes.

MAKES ABOUT 20 ½-CUP SERVINGS.

SHERRIED CHEESE MOLD

Pack this cheese mixture into a tower-shaped mold, and surround with crisp crackers. Very spreadable—and incredibly delicious!

½ pound American cheese, grated
¼ pound blue cheese, crumbled
1 3-ounce package cream cheese
½ cup sherry
½ teaspoon Worcestershire sauce
½ teaspoon paprika
½ teaspoon salt
½ teaspoon onion salt
Dash of garlic powder
Dash of cayenne

Have cheeses at room temperature. In a bowl, blend all cheeses well with a fork. Gradually beat in sherry and Worcestershire sauce, then add seasonings. Beat (preferably with an electric beater or blender) until mixture is smooth and creamy. Pack into a lightly oiled fancy mold, if desired. Store, covered, in the refrigerator.
MAKES 2½ CUPS OF SPREAD.

PUFFY SCRAMBLED EGGS

Start with a serving of melon and grapes, or any combination of fruits that are in season. Follow with two combination dishes below—each designed to please the palate in a festive way. Both will earn you a shower of praise!

1 5-serving envelope instant mashed
   potato granules
1½ teaspoons salt
1½ cups boiling water
1½ cups milk
8 eggs
¼ cup butter
Cherry tomatoes, if desired

Empty envelope of potato granules into a large mixing bowl; add salt and boiling water. With a fork, mix until the water is absorbed. Blend in milk, stirring until mixture is thick and smooth. Add eggs and beat thoroughly. Meanwhile melt butter in a large skillet over moderate heat. Pour potato-egg mixture into skillet. Cook slowly; as mixture sets, turn set portion over, using a pancake turner or large spoon. When egg is done, transfer to serving platter. Garnish with tomatoes. (Set platter on a warming tray, if it is not served at once.)
MAKES 8 SERVINGS.

CHICKEN SUPREME

4 whole chicken breasts, about 1 pound each
6 tablespoons butter
1 1¼-ounce envelope chicken gravy mix
1 6-ounce can sliced mushrooms
Water
1 teaspoon instant minced onion
Salt and pepper

Bone chicken breasts; remove skin; cut each breast half into 5 or 6 pieces. Melt butter in a skillet over moderately high heat. Add chicken pieces; cook, stirring constantly until all pieces have lost their pink color (about 4 minutes). Remove from heat; sprinkle chicken with gravy mix directly from the envelope. Drain liquid from the can of mushrooms into a measuring cup; add water to measure 1 cup. Pour liquid over chicken; add drained mushrooms and onion. Place over moderate heat; stir to blend smoothly as it comes to a boil. Simmer over low heat about 5 minutes. Add salt and pepper to taste.

MAKES 8 SERVINGS.

SESAME TRIANGLES

Fresh baked Sesame Triangles? Whenever did you find the time to do it? With a refrigerated roll head start, anyone can fit this goodie into a menu! Serve with fruity jam and watch them disappear.

1 can refrigerator crescent rolls
1 egg yolk
1 tablespoon milk
1 tablespoon sesame seeds

Unroll dough and separate into the 8 marked triangles; cut each triangle in half, making two smaller triangles. Place on

a lightly greased cookie sheet. With a fork, beat together the egg yolk and milk; brush each triangle with this mixture, then sprinkle with sesame seeds. Bake in a 375° oven for 8–10 minutes, or until lightly browned.
MAKES 16 TRIANGLES.

ORANGE PIE

A cookie crumb crust is used to cradle the fluffiest orange filling to satisfy mid-morning cravings. Garnish with fresh orange slices and serve in thin wedges —then do get on with the fun of opening the baby presents!

1⅓ cups chocolate wafer cookie crumbs
¼ cup melted butter
½ cup sugar
3 eggs, separated
2 teaspoons grated orange rind
½ cup fresh orange juice
3 tablespoons confectioner's sugar
1 cup heavy cream, whipped
Orange slices

Combine cookie crumbs with melted butter; press mixture firmly against sides and bottom of 9-inch pie plate. Bake at 375° for 8 minutes. Cool.

In 1-quart saucepan, combine ½ cup sugar with egg yolks, orange rind, and juice. Cook over low heat, stirring constantly, until mixture thickens and coats the spoon, about 5 minutes. Cool. Beat egg whites until foamy. Gradually beat in confectioner's sugar; continue beating until egg whites are stiff but not dry. Fold into cooked orange mixture; then fold in whipped cream. Lightly spoon filling into cookie crumb crust. Freeze until firm. Remove from freezer a few minutes before serving. Garnish pie with fresh orange slices.
MAKES 8 SERVINGS.

Orange Baskets and Crab Quiche.

HOUSEWARMING BRUNCH

As soon as you've unpacked the last box, invite your friends to a House-warming Brunch. There's nothing like giving a party to make you feel at home!

MENU

On arrival:
MULLED WINE*
MIXED NUTS

At the table:
ORANGE BASKETS*
CRAB QUICHE*
MIXED GREEN SALAD
OLIVES
HOT CROSS BUNS

For dessert:
APPLESAUCE SOUFFLÉ*
COFFEE

* Recipe follows

MULLED WINE

Your guests will really feel warmed when you serve them mugs of Mulled Wine. Accompany the wine with a large bowl of help-yourself mixed nuts. Serve with individual cinnamon sticks for swizzling!

1 cup sugar
4 cups water
Rind from half a lemon
18 whole cloves
2 3-inch cinnamon sticks
2 bottles burgundy or other red dinner
  wine

Dissolve sugar in water in large saucepan. Add strips of lemon rind, cloves, and cinnamon. Boil 15 minutes, then strain out peel and spices. Add wine and heat gently. Do not boil. Meanwhile, preheat the punch bowl or serving decanter by filling it with warm, then hot, water. When ready to serve, empty water from container and dry it. Pour in the mulled wine and serve immediately.
MAKES 20 SERVINGS.

ORANGE BASKETS

Pretty as a picture, these Orange Baskets are a nutritious beginning for your brunch. Follow it with a Crab Quiche for every four guests. Get the Hot Cross Buns from your local bakery or do-it-yourself with a mix!

8 large unblemished oranges
1 16-ounce can grapefruit sections
1 8¾-ounce can seedless grapes
1 13½-ounce can pineapple chunks
Maraschino cherries (optional)

Cut slice from top of each orange. Use zigzag cuts to decorate top rim of oranges. Hollow out oranges and cut pulp into cubes. In bowl, mix orange cubes, grapefruit sections, grapes, and pineapple chunks. Drain excess juice into pitcher to use as base for fruit drink. Spoon mixed fruit into orange baskets and decorate with maraschino cherries, if desired.
MAKES 8 SERVINGS.

CRAB QUICHE

2 7½-ounce cans Alaskan king crab, drained
3 tablespoons dry vermouth
3 tablespoons fresh parsley, finely chopped
½ teaspoon salt
¼ teaspoon pepper
2 eggs
½ cup milk
1 unbaked 9-inch pie shell

Place crab meat in a bowl and shred. Sprinkle with vermouth, parsley, salt, and pepper. Let stand for 15 minutes. Beat eggs and milk together. Pour crab meat mixture into unbaked pie shell. Pour egg mixture over crab meat. Bake at 350° for about 50 minutes, or until knife inserted into center comes out clean.
MAKES 4–6 SERVINGS AS A MAIN COURSE.

APPLESAUCE SOUFFLÉ

This "soufflé" is a fabulous fake! The fluffy mixture firms up in the refrigerator until serving time. A cool dessert for a housewarming!

3 3¾-ounce packages lemon-flavored whipped dessert mix
1½ cups cold milk
1½ cups cold pineapple juice
1½ cups applesauce
1 teaspoon apple pie spice
⅓ cup finely chopped maraschino cherries
½ cup whipping cream

Prepare dessert mix according to package directions, using cold milk and pineapple juice. Fold in applesauce, apple pie spice, and cherries. Make a foil collar about 3 inches wide around the top of a 1-quart soufflé dish. Pour mixture into dish; chill until firm. Whip cream. Decorate the top of the soufflé with sweetened whipped cream piped out of a pastry bag with a rosette tip.

MAKES 10–12 SERVINGS.

ANNIVERSARY BRUNCH

Celebrate your own anniversary or that of a friend with an invitation for brunch. Include all those who care, and serve a menu that becomes a memory. The food is frankly fancy!

MENU

On arrival:
ROYAL PEACH CHAMPAGNE PUNCH*
or
MINTED ORANGE JUICE

At the table:
MUSHROOM-CHIVE SCRAMBLE*
CHICKEN LIVER KABOBS*
SHRIMP TUREEN*
SURPRISE CORN MUFFINS*

For dessert:
POTS DE CRÈME*
ANNIVERSARY CAKE
COFFEE

Recipe follows

ROYAL PEACH CHAMPAGNE PUNCH

Toast the happy milestone with this conversation piece punch. Fresh peaches ooze their sweet juice into the champagne mixture, and guests scoop up fresh strawberries into every glass. Set out nuts and nibbles for those who need sustenance before brunch!

3 ripe peaches, unpeeled
Ice block
1 bottle aurora sauterne
1 teaspoon angostura bitters
2 bottles brut champagne
1 quart fresh whole strawberries,
    washed

Pierce whole peaches deeply and thoroughly with a fork. Place them in the bottom of the punch bowl and lay a block of ice on top of them. Combine sauterne and bitters; pour into punch bowl. Add champagne and strawberries.
MAKES ABOUT 25 PUNCH-CUP SERVINGS.

MUSHROOM-CHIVE SCRAMBLE

Cream and eggs combine with mushrooms and chives to cook into a glamour version of scrambled eggs. Keep it hot in a chafing dish until ready to serve. Garnish each portion with a skewered Chicken Liver Kabob—great tastes for a great day!

1 6-ounce package frozen whole
mushrooms in butter sauce
16 large eggs
1 cup light cream
1½ teaspoons salt
½ teaspoon pepper
4 teaspoons chopped chives
¼ cup butter

Remove frozen mushrooms from pouch; place in a medium-size saucepan. Cover and place over high heat for 5 minutes. Remove cover; reduce heat. Continue cooking, tossing lightly with fork, until butter sauce is absorbed and mushrooms are golden brown.

Combine eggs with cream, salt, pepper, and chives. Melt butter in large skillet; pour in eggs. Cook over low heat, stirring occasionally, until eggs are thickened but still moist. Stir in mushrooms, reserving a few for garnish. MAKES 8 SERVINGS.

CHICKEN LIVER KABOBS

8 strips bacon
8 chicken livers, cut in halves
16 cherry tomatoes

Starting with bacon, loosely thread 2 chicken liver halves and 2 tomatoes on eight 8-inch metal skewers, weaving bacon over and under pieces. Broil 5–6 inches from heat for 10–15 minutes, turning occasionally, until livers and bacon are done. MAKES 8 SERVINGS.

SHRIMP TUREEN

Ladle a splendid shrimp and vegetable mixture into baked pastry tarts, on toast points, or in scooped-out English muffin halves. Offer a basket of tiny hot corn muffins—with surprise ingredients—and pass the butter. Who diets on a happy day anyway?

1 10-ounce package frozen baby peas in butter sauce
3 tablespoons butter
3 tablespoons flour
1½ cups half-and-half cream
1 cup shredded American cheese
1 7-ounce can artichoke hearts, drained and cut in quarters
1 4½-ounce can shrimp, drained
3 tablespoons cooking sherry
½ teaspoon salt
Dash of pepper
Pastry tarts, toast points, or toasted English muffins

Cook peas according to package directions. In medium saucepan, melt butter and blend in flour. Gradually stir in half-and-half. Cook over medium heat, stirring constantly until thickened. Add cheese, stirring until melted. Stir in peas in butter sauce and artichoke hearts, shrimp, sherry, salt, and pepper.
MAKES 8 SERVINGS.

SURPRISE CORN MUFFINS

1 7½-ounce package corn muffin mix
1 7-ounce can golden whole kernel corn
   with red and green sweet peppers,
   drained

Prepare corn muffin mix as directed on the package. Stir in drained corn. Spoon into paper-lined or well-greased tiny muffin cups. Bake at 400° for 12–15 minutes.
MAKES ABOUT 18 TINY MUFFINS.

POTS DE CRÈME

Tiny Pots de Crème provide just enough chocolate to satisfy your sweet tooth. Follow these with an anniversary cake from the bakery, or simply stick a tiny candle into each cup of chocolate and let each guest make a wish for the happy couple and blow it out!

8 ounces sweet chocolate candy bar
½ pound butter, very soft
1 tablespoon sugar
5 egg whites
Grated coconut (optional)

Melt the chocolate in the top of a double boiler. Remove from heat. Mix thoroughly with soft butter. Add sugar. Beat egg whites until thick and standing in peaks; fold in the chocolate mixture. Pour into china pots and refrigerate until firm. Top with a sprinkling of grated coconut if desired.
MAKES 8 SERVINGS.

Seagoing Shrimp Salad, Deviled Eggs,
and Date and Nut Bread.

BON VOYAGE BRUNCH

Give a traveler you know a send-off to remember. It will make the trip exciting even before it begins! Just to get in the mood, several menu items are from the deep blue sea. For ease of planning, the entire menu can make an overnight stop in the refrigerator.

MENU

On arrival:
HOT CLAM AND TOMATO BOUILLON*
TUNA TEASERS*

At the table:
SEAGOING SHRIMP SALAD*
DEVILED EGGS*
CARROT CURLS
GREEN PEAS

For dessert:
DATE AND NUT BREAD*
MINTED ICED TEA

Recipe follows

HOT CLAM AND TOMATO BOUILLON

Hand each guest a mug of hot soup on arrival and let him help himself to appetizers. It'll be clear sailing from then on!

1 46-ounce can clam and tomato juice
2 10½-ounce cans beef bouillon
1 cup popped corn

Combine juice and bouillon in a saucepan; heat through. Serve hot in large mugs. Garnish each mug of hot soup with a few kernels of popped corn.
MAKES 8–10 SERVINGS.

TUNA TEASERS

1 7-ounce can tuna, drained
¼ cup chutney
2 tablespoons mayonnaise
2 teaspoons grated Parmesan cheese
2 dozen crisp crackers
Paprika

Mash tuna; add chutney, mayonnaise, and cheese. Mix thoroughly. Spoon onto crackers; dash paprika over top of each. Slip under the broiler just before serving, until bubbly hot.
MAKES 24 APPETIZERS.

SEAGOING SHRIMP SALAD

Tomato sauce with cheese already added gives this molded shrimp salad its pretty pink color and piquant flavor. Surround it with deviled eggs and crisp carrot curls. Place peas around the base of the mold to give a green nest effect!

1 envelope unflavored gelatin
1 tablespoon lemon juice
⅓ cup boiling water
1 8-ounce can tomato sauce with cheese
½ cup sour cream
½ cup mayonnaise
2 cups cleaned cooked shrimp
2 10-ounce packages frozen peas,
  cooked and drained
1 4½-ounce can ripe olives, drained
  and sliced
½ teaspoon basil
Lettuce

Soften gelatin in lemon juice; add water and stir until dissolved. Blend in tomato sauce with cheese, sour cream, and mayonnaise. Fold in shrimp, 1 cup peas, olives, and basil. Pour into 1½-quart mold. Chill until set. Unmold on chilled serving plate and garnish with lettuce and remaining peas. MAKES 8 SERVINGS.

DEVILED EGGS

8 hard-cooked eggs, peeled
¼ cup mayonnaise
1 teaspoon prepared mustard
½ teaspoon salt
¼ teaspoon pepper
Paprika

Cut eggs in halves lengthwise. Remove yolks and mash with mayonnaise, mustard, salt, and pepper. Fill egg-whites with the mixture, swirling the tops with the tines of a fork. Dash paprika over each. MAKES 16 PIECES.

DATE AND NUT BREAD

Have plenty of softened cream cheese on hand to slather over slices of fresh-baked Date and Nut Bread, and count on seconds of coffee with it. What a satisfying way to say, "Have a good trip."

1 cup boiling water
1 cup dates, pitted and coarsely chopped
½ cup seedless raisins
1 egg, beaten
½ cup brown sugar
1½ cups flour
1 teaspoon baking powder
1 teaspoon baking soda
½ teaspoon salt
1 cup broken walnuts or pecans

Pour boiling water over dates and raisins; stir and let cool. When mixture is cool, beat egg, add sugar, and then add date and raisin mixture. Sift flour, baking powder, baking soda, and salt. Add to egg mixture, leaving about ½ cup of flour mixture to be mixed with broken nuts. Add floured nuts to mixture. Bake in greased loaf pan at 350° for 45–60 minutes. Test for doneness with a toothpick; when dough no longer sticks to wood and is well browned, it is done.
SERVES 8–12.

WELCOME HOME BRUNCH

*Give a hearty welcome home to some-
one you love by inviting friends to share
the moment. This menu says that you
really care!*

MENU

On arrival:
TOMATO JUICE WITH LIME WEDGES
CHICKEN LIVER-BACON ROLLS*

At the table:
BROCCOLI OMELET WITH
MUSHROOM SAUCE*
LAYERED GLAZED HAM*

For dessert:
MACAROON COFFEE CAKE*
COFFEE

* Recipe follows

CHICKEN LIVER-BACON ROLLS

Chopped chicken livers and rice are wrapped in bacon for a toothsome treat. Just a sample of the other goodies to come!

½ pound chicken livers
2 tablespoons butter
½ cup tomato juice
1 egg, well beaten
½ cup dry bread crumbs
1 cup cooked rice
½ teaspoon celery salt
Dash of pepper
½ teaspoon onion powder
12 slices bacon, cut in halves, crosswise

Sauté chicken livers in butter until tender. Chop fine. Mix tomato juice and egg; add crumbs, rice, celery salt, pepper, and onion powder. Add chopped livers. Mix thoroughly. Roll into finger lengths; wrap each roll with ½ slice bacon and fasten with wooden picks. Place on a rack in a shallow baking pan. Bake at 425° for 10–15 minutes, or until bacon is well done. Serve hot.

MAKES 2 DOZEN ROLLS.

BROCCOLI OMELET
WITH MUSHROOM SAUCE

*You will equate omelets with elegance
once you have tasted this baked broccoli
puff. Do make two of them if you are
planning to serve eight to twelve guests
—there'll be nothing left but a round
of compliments!*

6 eggs, separated
⅓ cup milk
½ cup finely chopped cooked broccoli
½ teaspoon salt
Dash pepper
3 tablespoons butter
⅓ cup chopped onion
⅛ teaspoon crushed leaf marjoram
2 tablespoons butter
1 10½-ounce can mushroom gravy
2 tablespoons sour cream
¼ teaspoon lemon juice

Beat egg whites until stiff. Beat yolks until thick and lemon-colored; mix in milk, broccoli, salt, and pepper. Fold yolk mixture into whites. Melt 3 tablespoons butter in a 10-inch ovenproof skillet; pour egg mixture into the hot butter. Cook over low heat until brown underneath (about 5 minutes). Bake at 350° for 15–20 minutes, or until surface is dry and center springs back when pressed lightly. Meanwhile, in a saucepan, cook onion with marjoram in the remaining 2 tablespoons butter until tender; add mushroom gravy, sour cream, and lemon juice. Heat; stir now and then. Serve with omelet.

MAKES 4–6 SERVINGS.

LAYERED GLAZED HAM

Here's an easy ham for the hostess to serve. It's sliced before baking, then coated with a wine glaze during cooking. Do use one of our native California wines for a delightful taste!

1 fully cooked boneless ham (may be canned), about 8 pounds
½ cup rosé wine
½ cup orange juice
½ cup brown sugar
¼ cup honey
2 tablespoons wine vinegar
¼ teaspoon cloves
¼ teaspoon ginger
2 teaspoons grated orange rind
1 teaspoon cornstarch

Have butcher slice and tie ham back together. Bake in a 325° oven about 2 hours, or until well heated. Meanwhile, combine wine, orange juice, brown sugar, honey, vinegar, cloves, ginger, orange rind, and cornstarch. Simmer together 5 minutes. When ready to glaze ham, increase oven temperature to 400°. Spoon glaze on ham every 10 minutes for about ½ hour. Serve ham hot or cold.
MAKES 12–16 SERVINGS.

MACAROON COFFEE CAKE

For a deliciously different coffee cake, try making this macaroon-filled star. Fortunately, it makes two, one for brunch and one to tuck into the freezer for another festive occasion. What a way to welcome someone home!

¾ cup water
¼ cup milk
¼ cup instant mashed potato granules
1 package active dry yeast
½ cup warm water
1 cup sour cream
⅔ cup shortening
½ cup sugar
1½ teaspoons salt
2 eggs, slightly beaten
6–7 cups all-purpose flour
Macaroon filling (recipe follows)

Combine ¾ cup water and the milk in small saucepan; heat to boiling. Remove from heat and stir in potato granules; whip lightly with fork until fluffy. Cool. Sprinkle yeast over ½ cup warm water; stir to dissolve. Combine sour cream, shortening, sugar, salt, and potatoes in large mixing bowl. Add dissolved yeast, eggs, and 3 cups flour; beat until smooth. Stir in remaining flour until mixture forms a stiff dough. Knead on floured surface 10–15 minutes until smooth and elastic. Place dough in greased mixing bowl; turn dough in bowl to grease all surfaces. Cover and let rise in warm place until light and double in size, 30 to 40 minutes. Punch down. Divide in half. Roll out half of dough to a 12-inch circle; place on well-greased baking sheet. Spread half the macaroon filling over circle to within 1 inch of outside edge. Starting at center of circle, cut 6 pie-shaped wedges just to edge of filling. Do not cut through. Roll each wedge, jelly-roll fashion, to center of ring. Pull edges of each roll outward, shaping with hands to form points, making star shape. Repeat with second half of dough. Cover both and let rise until light and double in size. Bake at 375° for 25–30 minutes until golden brown. MAKES 6–10 SERVINGS EACH.

Macaroon Filling

1 cup confectioner's sugar
1 cup crumbled coconut macaroons
½ cup soft butter
½ teaspoon almond extract

Combine sugar and crumbled macaroons. Add softened butter and work through. Add almond extract.

Eggs in Rice Rings with Cheddar Sauce.

GUEST OF HONOR BRUNCH

For that special someone who merits your attention, give a Guest of Honor Brunch. Then serve beautiful food and bask in the reflection of warm compliments. Here's a menu that honors your guest.

MENU

On arrival:
CITRUS FIZZ*
STUFFED PRUNES*

At the table:
EGGS IN RICE RINGS WITH
CHEDDAR SAUCE*
POACHED SALMON STEAKS*
SLICED CUCUMBERS

For dessert:
CINNAMON-RAISIN BRUNCH BREAD*
COFFEE

* Recipe follows

CITRUS FIZZ

This Citrus Fizz combines fruit juice concentrates to make a tingly midmorning drink. Serve it with a platter of stuffed prunes which were made a week ahead so the wine filling has a chance to ripen. A sweet beginning to a sweet gesture!

1 6-ounce can frozen orange juice concentrate, thawed
¼ cup frozen grapefruit juice concentrate, thawed
¼ cup frozen limeade concentrate, thawed
1 quart ginger ale
Ice cubes
Fruit wedges (optional)

Blend undiluted concentrates in a large pitcher. Just before serving, add ginger ale and ice cubes. Pour into short wide glasses (old-fashioneds) and decorate with wedges of peeled orange and other fruit on food picks, if desired.
MAKES 8–10 SERVINGS.

STUFFED PRUNES

36 prunes
½ cup ground walnuts
½ cup ground mixed glacé fruit (prepared fruitcake mix)
¼ cup port wine
Dash of cinnamon
Dash of nutmeg
Dash of salt
Granulated sugar

Place prunes in a colander over boiling water; cover and steam 10–15 minutes, or until soft. Dry prunes well. Slit lengthwise and remove pits. Press two prunes together end to

end with edges overlapping slightly to make 18 double-length prunes. Mix walnuts, glacé fruit, wine, cinnamon, nutmeg, and salt. Stuff the double prunes with this mixture. Roll in sugar. Store in a tightly covered container at room temperature, and let ripen for a week or more before serving.
MAKES 18 STUFFED PRUNES.

EGGS IN RICE RINGS WITH CHEDDAR SAUCE

Be sure to keep these rice rings hot on a warming tray while you poach the eggs to slip into the centers. A quick-trick Cheddar Sauce can be spooned over each serving by the guests. Pretty as a picture and a taste treat, too!

4 cups cooked rice
2 10½-ounce cans condensed cream of
    mushroom soup
8 slices bacon, cooked and crumbled
1½ cups diced Cheddar cheese
8 poached eggs (recipe follows)
Salt and pepper to taste
½ cup milk

Mix cooked rice with ¾ of a can of condensed mushroom soup, crumbled bacon, and ¾ cup diced cheese. Heat and stir until cheese is melted. Press into 8 individual rings and turn onto serving plates. Place a poached egg in the center of each. Season with salt and pepper. Combine remaining soup with milk and remaining cheese; heat and stir until cheese is melted. Place in a sauceboat to be passed at the table.
MAKES 8 SERVINGS.

Continued on next page

EGGS IN RICE RINGS WITH CHEDDAR SAUCE/Continued

Poached Eggs

Fill a skillet with two inches of water, bringing it to a rolling boil. Reduce heat to simmer, add a teaspoon of vinegar, and break each egg carefully into the water. If white spreads, push it toward the center with a spoon. Cook for 4 minutes or less depending on desired doneness. Remove egg with a slotted spoon and trim edges with kitchen shears, if desired.

POACHED SALMON STEAKS

Poached Salmon Steak may be served hot or cold. Either way it's a perfect pink delicacy for your special guest. Stir a few capers into mayonnaise-type salad dressing for those who prefer a sauce. Garnish with cucumber slices—run the tines of a fork down the sides before you slice and you will have scalloped edges for a prettier effect!

8 1-inch-thick slices salmon steak
Boiling water
1 tablespoon tarragon vinegar
1 teaspoon salt
6 whole black peppercorns

Arrange salmon slices in a large skillet. (You may need two skillets.) Add enough boiling water to cover fish. Add vinegar, salt, and peppercorns. Simmer for about 10 minutes, or until salmon is tender but still holds its shape. Remove carefully and serve hot, or refrigerate and serve cold.
MAKES 8 SERVINGS.

CINNAMON-RAISIN BRUNCH BREAD

Baking your own brunch bread for dessert becomes a pleasure with this simple recipe. Serve it warm from the oven, and pass some orange marmalade, if desired. Have plenty of coffee on hand, for this is the kind of brunch dessert to linger over!

1 cup sifted all-purpose flour
2½ teaspoons baking powder
½ teaspoon salt
1 teaspoon cinnamon
1 cup whole bran cereal
¾ cup milk
½ cup soft shortening
½ cup sugar
2 eggs
1 cup seedless raisins
½ cup chopped nuts
2 tablespoons sugar
¼ teaspoon cinnamon

Sift together flour, baking powder, salt, and 1 teaspoon cinnamon; set aside. Combine cereal and milk; let stand until most of moisture is absorbed. Measure shortening, ½ cup sugar, and eggs into a mixing bowl; beat until light and fluffy. Stir in cereal mixture, raisins, and nuts. Add sifted dry ingredients, stirring until combined. Spread in greased 9-inch layer cake pan. Mix 2 tablespoons sugar and ¼ teaspoon cinnamon for topping; sprinkle evenly over brunch bread. Bake in 375° oven for 30 minutes, or until lightly browned. Serve warm, cut in wedges.
MAKES 8–10 SERVINGS.

Chocolate Cloud Pie.

BRIDGE BRUNCH

You may not get a decent bridge hand, but here's a grand slam menu to serve before your guests get serious at the card table. No need to be defensive about the scrumptious chocolate pie— even dieting guests will not have the willpower to say, "I pass."

MENU

On arrival:
APRICOT NECTAR
SHERRIED CHEESE CRACKERS*

At the table:
FROSTY SHRIMP SOUP*
EGGS BENEDICT*
STUFFED TOMATOES*

For dessert:
CHOCOLATE CLOUD PIE*
COFFEE

* Recipe follows

SHERRIED CHEESE CRACKERS

Serve chilled apricot nectar in long-stemmed wine glasses. Prepare the Sherried Cheese Crackers beforehand, so they will be ready to slip under the broiler. A subtle start to a pleasant afternoon.

1 tablespoon butter
¾ cup grated Cheddar cheese
2 tablespoons sherry
2 teaspoons chopped chives
16 large round sesame seed crackers

Cream butter; add cheese, sherry, and chives and mix well. Mound mixture on the crackers and place on a baking sheet. Slip under the broiler for 5 minutes, or until cheese topping is browned. Serve at once.
MAKES 16 CRACKERS.

FROSTY SHRIMP SOUP

Be sure to make this soup long before your guests arrive—preferably the day before—so it will be frosty cold at serving time. It's a lovely contrast to the hot dish that follows.

1 cup cooked rice
2 cups hot chicken broth
1 10-ounce can condensed frozen shrimp soup, thawed
⅓ cup canned tomatoes and green chilies
1 cup sour cream
Chopped chives

Combine rice and chicken broth in electric blender; blend until rice has a smooth consistency. Add soup and tomatoes and green chilies; continue blending until all ingredients are smooth. Chill until frosty cold. Serve in small soup cups or bowls. Float a dollop of sour cream topped with chives in each serving of soup. MAKES 8 SERVINGS.

EGGS BENEDICT

Make your own fresh Hollandaise Sauce using the recipe below, and spoon over poached eggs—making a perfect brunch dish of Eggs Benedict. The stuffed tomatoes on the side will earn you no trump applause!

8 whole eggs
8 slices cooked ham
4 English muffins, halved and toasted
Hollandaise Sauce (recipe follows)

Poach eggs (follow directions on page 100, Guest of Honor Brunch); gently remove poached eggs from skillet with a slotted spoon. Place ham on toasted muffins; top with a poached egg on each; spoon Hollandise Sauce over each egg. MAKES 8 SERVINGS.

Hollandaise Sauce

2 egg yolks
¼ teaspoon salt
¼ teaspoon Tabasco sauce
½ cup melted butter
1 tablespoon fresh lemon juice

Beat egg yolks, salt, and Tabasco until thick and lemon-colored. Add ¼ cup hot melted butter, about 1 teaspoon at a time, beating constantly. Combine remaining butter with lemon juice. Add slowly, beating constantly. Cover, and set aside in a pan over hot water until needed, stirring occasionally.

STUFFED TOMATOES

1 17-ounce can early peas, drained
¾ cup diced mild American cheese
⅔ cup diced dill pickle
½ cup mayonnaise
8 large ripe tomatoes
Salt
Lettuce

Combine peas, diced cheese, and diced pickle; toss with mayonnaise. Cut the tops off the stem end of the tomatoes; scoop out the centers, cut up meaty pieces and mix with peas. Sprinkle the insides of tomatoes with salt; then stuff with pea mixture. Serve on a lettuce leaf.
MAKES 8 SERVINGS.

CHOCOLATE CLOUD PIE

A layer of meringue is baked in the crust of this feather-light pie. Then alternate layers of chocolate fluff and whipped cream form the filling. Eight hearts are going to love this dessert!

Crust

1 cup sifted all-purpose flour
¾ teaspoon salt
⅓ cup shortening
3 or 4 tablespoons cold water
2 egg whites
½ teaspoon vinegar
¼ teaspoon cinnamon
½ cup sugar

Combine flour and ½ teaspoon salt in a mixing bowl; cut in shortening until it is the consistency of coarse meal. Sprinkle water, 1 tablespoon at a time, over mixture, tossing quickly and lightly with a fork until dough is just moist enough to hold together. Roll out pastry to fit a 9-inch pie plate. Fit pastry gently into plate. Prick generously with a fork. Bake in a 450° oven for 12 minutes, or until golden brown. Beat together egg whites, vinegar, cinnamon, and remaining ¼ teaspoon salt until stiff but not dry. Gradually add sugar and beat until very stiff. Spread meringue over bottom and up sides of baked pastry shell. Bake in a slow oven (325°) for 15–18 minutes, or until lightly browned. Cool.

Filling

1 cup semisweet chocolate morsels
2 egg yolks
¼ cup water
1 cup heavy cream
¼ cup sugar
¼ teaspoon cinnamon

Melt semisweet chocolate morsels over hot (not boiling) water. Blend in egg yolks and water until smooth. Spread 3 tablespoons chocolate mixture over cooled meringue; chill remainder until it begins to thicken. Beat together heavy cream, sugar, and cinnamon until whipped and thick. Spread ½ whipped cream mixture over chocolate layer in pie shell. Fold chilled chocolate mixture into remaining whipped cream mixture. Spread over whipped cream in pie shell. Chill pie at least 4 hours before serving.
MAKES 8 SERVINGS.

Pickles with Curried Dip, Pickles in a Blanket,
and Football Hamburgers.

BEFORE THE GAME BRUNCH

To get in the rah rah spirit, plan a quick and satisfying brunch before the football game. Send an extra thermos of hot coffee along with the cheering section and they might give a yell just for you!

MENU

On arrival:
CIDER
PICKLES IN A BLANKET*
PICKLES WITH CURRIED DIP*

At the table:
FOOTBALL HAMBURGERS*
SAUERKRAUT-RAISIN BAKE*
POTATO CHIPS

For dessert:
APPLESAUCE DOUGHNUTS*
COFFEE

* Recipe follows

PICKLES IN A BLANKET

Start the pregame formation with plenty of pickles for all. Wrap some in blankets of dried beef, and have others just for dunking in Curried Dip. Kicks the day off to a good beginning!

12 slices dried beef
12 dill pickles, quartered lengthwise
Mustard

Soak dried beef in water and dry on paper towels. Cut each slice in four strips. Roll beef strips around quartered pickles and fasten with toothpicks. Serve mustard for those who desire it.
MAKES 36 PIECES.

PICKLES WITH CURRIED DIP

2 cups mayonnaise
2 tablespoons curry
Pickle quarters and sweet chips

Combine mayonnaise and curry; let stand an hour. Serve as a dip with pickles.
MAKES 2 CUPS OF DIP.

FOOTBALL HAMBURGERS

There's a Cheddar cheese surprise in the center of each football at this game —good enough to score a touchdown with every tastebud.

2 pounds ground beef
2 eggs
½ teaspoon salt
¼ teaspoon pepper
8 ½-inch cubes Cheddar cheese
1 3-ounce package cream cheese
2 tablespoons milk

Mix ground meat with eggs, salt, and pepper. Divide meat in 8 parts. Wrap each cube of Cheddar cheese with ground meat mixture and shape into a football. Broil "footballs" until desired degree of doneness is reached. Soften cream cheese with milk and place mixture in a cake decorating tube; decorate footballs quickly with mixture to look like laces.
MAKES 8 HAMBURGERS.

SAUERKRAUT-RAISIN BAKE

4 cups sauerkraut
½ cup thinly sliced onions
1 teaspoon caraway seeds
2 small apples, diced and cored
1 cup raisins
3 tablespoons brown sugar
½ cup water

Combine sauerkraut, onions, and caraway seeds. Add diced apples, raisins, and 2 tablespoons of the brown sugar. Mix well. Turn into a greased 1½-quart casserole and sprinkle top with remaining tablespoon of brown sugar. Pour water over contents of casserole. Cover and bake at 350° for 40 minutes, or until apples are tender.
MAKES 8 SERVINGS.

APPLESAUCE DOUGHNUTS

*Make your own doughnuts? Why not—
when they are as easy as the recipe below. There's enough to send along in a
"care package" for nibblers at the game!*

3 eggs
1 cup sugar
1 cup canned applesauce
2 teaspoons grated lemon rind
2 tablespoons melted shortening
4 cups sifted all-purpose flour
1 teaspoon baking soda
1½ teaspoons baking powder
½ teaspoon nutmeg
1 teaspoon salt
Confectioner's sugar (optional)

Beat eggs, gradually add sugar, beating constantly. Add applesauce, lemon rind, and shortening. Sift together flour, baking
soda, baking powder, nutmeg, and salt; add to first mixture.
Mix well. Place dough in waxed paper; chill. Roll out ½ inch
thick on lightly floured board. Cut out doughnuts with floured
cutter. Fry in deep fat, heated to 375°, for 3 minutes, turning
until golden brown. Drain on absorbent paper. Dip in confectioner's sugar, if desired.
MAKES 36 PIECES.

GRADUATION BRUNCH

Make this graduation day one to remember by celebrating with a brunch that's sure to please. Someone may award you a special diploma for Menu Magician of the year!

MENU

On arrival:
APPLE POLISHER'S COCKTAIL*
BLUE CHEESE TURNOVERS*

At the table:
DEVILED SCRAMBLED EGGS*
GLAZED BRUNCH LOAF*
SAUTERNE ASPIC*
CRESCENT ROLLS

For dessert:
FRUIT FLOAT*
COFFEE

Recipe follows

APPLE POLISHER'S COCKTAIL

Here's an amusing Apple Polisher's Cocktail to honor the hard-earned sheepskin. Serve it with Blue Cheese Turnovers—a quick-trick recipe that deserves an honorary degree!

½ cube sugar
3 ounces apple juice
3 dashes grenadine
1 teaspoon lemon juice

In each tall-stemmed glass, combine ingredients and stir. Serve at once.
MAKES 1 DRINK.

BLUE CHEESE TURNOVERS

2 ounces blue cheese
2 ounces cream cheese
1 egg, beaten
1 10-ounce package pie crust mix
    (or pastry for two 9-inch pie crusts)
2 tablespoons jellied cranberry sauce

Combine blue cheese, cream cheese, and half of egg. Beat until smooth. Prepare pie crust dough; roll out on a floured board to ⅛-inch thickness. Cut into 2-inch squares. Place ¼ teaspoon cheese mixture and ⅛ teaspoon cranberry sauce on each square. Brush edges with a little egg, fold into a triangle and press edges together with a fork. Slit top of each and brush with remaining egg. Place on greased cookie sheet. Bake at 375° about 10 minutes. Serve hot or cold.
MAKES ABOUT 48 TURNOVERS.

DEVILED SCRAMBLED EGGS

These scrambled eggs have a flavor of distinction. Serve them with slices of Glazed Brunch Loaf, which boasts a fruit topping. Both will pass the taste test with top grades!

8 eggs, slightly beaten
1 4-ounce can sliced mushrooms, drained
¼ cup prepared yellow mustard
2 tablespoons chopped green onions
1 teaspoon Worcestershire sauce
½ teaspoon salt
2 tablespoons butter

Combine eggs, mushrooms, mustard, onions, Worcestershire sauce, and salt. Melt butter in skillet; add egg mixture. Cook over low heat until eggs are set, but still glossy and moist, stirring occasionally with a spatula. Serve at once.
MAKES 4 SERVINGS.

GLAZED BRUNCH LOAF

¼ cup apricot preserves
2 tablespoons drained crushed pineapple
2 teaspoons Worcestershire sauce
1 12-ounce can luncheon loaf

Combine preserves, pineapple, and Worcestershire sauce; pour over loaf. Bake in a 350° oven for 20 minutes.
MAKES 4 SERVINGS.

SAUTERNE ASPIC

Get an "A" for aspic-making with this crunchy sauterne-flavored marvel. A few drops of green coloring will make the mayonnaise dressing look like a surprise topping—a little flair without fuss!

2 envelopes unflavored gelatin
¼ cup lemon juice
2½ cups tomato juice
1 cup sauterne (or other white dinner wine)
½ teaspoon salt
½ teaspoon Worcestershire sauce
⅛ teaspoon Tabasco sauce
4 small green onions
1 medium-sized cucumber
½ cup chopped green pepper
1½ cups chopped celery
Salad greens
Mayonnaise
Few drops green food coloring (optional)

Soften gelatin in lemon juice. Heat tomato juice to simmering, add softened gelatin and stir until it is dissolved. Blend in sauterne, salt, Worcestershire sauce, and Tabasco. Cool until slightly thickened. Meanwhile, slice onions thin, and peel and dice cucumber. Combine with green pepper and chopped celery. Fold into thickened gelatin and pour into 1½-quart mold. Chill until firm. Unmold onto crisp salad greens and serve with mayonnaise (colored green if desired).
MAKES 8–12 SERVINGS.

FRUIT FLOAT

Just in case you bet an ice cream soda that the graduate wouldn't make it— here's the perfect pay-off! It's a Fruit Float with a dash of rum to make it a memorable reward.

1 6-ounce can frozen concentrated
    orange juice
2 cups cold water
1½ pints vanilla ice cream
½ cup rum
1 12-ounce package frozen mixed fruit,
    thawed and drained
8 maraschino cherries

Mix orange juice and water. Gradually pour over ½ pint of the ice cream in a bowl, beating until thoroughly blended. Add the rum and mix well. Spoon the mixed fruit into 8 glasses. Pour in the orange juice mixture. Top each with a scoop of the remaining ice cream. Garnish with a maraschino cherry.

MAKES 8 SERVINGS.

Beef and Mushroom Fondue, and clockwise from top, Orange Ginger Sauce, Avocado Dill Sauce, and Blue Cheese Sauce.

FONDUE BRUNCH

This brunch menu requires at least three fondue pots—about par for the wedding gifts received these days. If you haven't received your due share, borrow them from your friends who have, and use them for an all-out, do-it-yourself meal. Fun with fondue from beginning to end!

MENU

On arrival:
CHILLED DRY WHITE WINE
CHEESE FONDUE*

At the table:
BEEF AND MUSHROOM FONDUE*
ORANGE GINGER SAUCE*
AVOCADO DILL SAUCE*
BLUE CHEESE SAUCE*

For dessert:
CHOCOLATE FONDUE*
COFFEE

* Recipe follows

CHEESE FONDUE

Tell your guests to keep stirring the appetizing Cheese Fondue in a figure-eight motion as they rotate their speared bread through the fondue pot. Keep your heat low for best results, and when all is done—divide the hardened disc at the bottom. A treat!

1 cut garlic clove
1 cup dry white wine
8 ounces gruyere cheese, cubed
2 tablespoons Kirsch
¼ teaspoon pepper
¼ teaspoon nutmeg
1 loaf French or Italian bread, cut in cubes

Rub interior of fondue pot with cut garlic clove; discard. Pour in wine, cubed cheese, and then Kirsch. Stir over low heat until cheese is melted and smooth. Add pepper and nutmeg. Keep warm over a candle warmer or other device to provide low heat. Serve with long fondue forks used to spear cubes of bread, which are then dunked into the fondue pot to be coated with cheese mixture.
SERVES 8 AS AN APPETIZER.

BEEF AND MUSHROOM FONDUE

Your guests will have a great time cooking strips of beef and fresh mushroom halves in sizzling butter and oil, sparked with fresh lemon juice. Three unusual dipping sauces keep the party perking!

2 parts salad oil
1 part butter
2 tablespoons freshly squeezed lemon
    juice
2 pounds round steak or sirloin tip, cut
    in thin 1-inch strips
1 pound fresh mushrooms, halved or
    quartered
Orange Ginger Sauce (recipe follows)
Avocado Dill Sauce (recipe follows)
Blue Cheese Sauce (recipe follows)

Heat enough oil and butter to half fill the fondue pot. Add
lemon juice. Heat to just below smoking point and keep oil
bubbling during cooking. Have beef strips and mushrooms
at room temperature and place on serving tray on table. Set
out small bowls of sauces.

Each guest spears a piece of beef or mushroom on a long
fondue fork or bamboo skewer, then holds it in the hot oil
until cooked to desired doneness, usually 30 to 60 seconds. He
then dips it in a sauce on his plate, eating at once.

Add more oil to pan as needed and skim surface of oil
occasionally.

SERVES 8.

Orange Ginger Sauce

½ cup mayonnaise
½ cup sour cream
1 teaspoon freshly grated orange rind
2 tablespoons orange juice
1 tablespoon finely chopped crystallized
    ginger
2 tablespoons finely chopped cashew
    nuts
1 clove garlic, crushed
1 teaspoon soy sauce

Combine all ingredients and mix well. Refrigerate 1 hour or
longer to blend flavors.

MAKES 1¼ CUPS SAUCE.

Continued on next page

BEEF AND MUSHROOM FONDUE/Continued

Avocado Dill Sauce

1 ripe avocado, mashed
½ teaspoon freshly grated lemon rind
2 teaspoons lemon juice
1 cup sour cream
1 teaspoon seasoned salt
¼ teaspoon dried dill weed, or more to taste

Combine avocado with lemon rind and juice. Blend in remaining ingredients. Chill.
MAKES 1½ CUPS SAUCE.

Blue Cheese Sauce

2 tablespoons crumbled blue cheese
2 tablespoons orange juice
2 teaspoons freshly grated orange rind
1 cup catsup
¼ teaspoon Worcestershire sauce
½ teaspoon grated horseradish

Mash blue cheese with orange juice. Add remaining ingredients and blend thoroughly. Allow to stand at least 1 hour before serving.
MAKES 1¼ CUPS SAUCE.

CHOCOLATE FONDUE

Dessert brings on still another fondue idea: Chocolate Fonduc with fruit and ladyfingers as the dippers. Again, keep it warm and pass the forks!

12 ounces Swiss milk chocolate
½ cup cream
2 tablespoons apricot brandy
2 bananas, peeled and cut in 1-inch slices
1 pint strawberries, cleaned
1 1-pound can pineapple spears, drained
1 package ladyfingers, split

Heat chocolate and cream together in a fondue pot until chocolate is melted and mixture is smooth. Add apricot brandy, and keep mixture warm for dipping. Arrange bananas, strawberries, pineapple spears, and lady fingers on a platter. Provide fondue forks and let your guests spear fruit or lady fingers on a fork, then dip into heated chocolate mixture. SERVES 8.

Eggs and Rice Supreme.

BARBECUE BRUNCH

Barbecue your brunch outdoors after an indoor head start with the preparations. Use paper plates and other toss-aways wherever you can to make cleanup time a matter of minutes!

MENU

On arrival:
PURPLE PUNCH*
CHEESE BURGERETTES*

At the table:
EGGS AND RICE SUPREME*
BEAN BAGS*

For dessert:
FROZEN LEMON PIE*
COFFEE

* Recipe follows

PURPLE PUNCH

Float a cherry-filled ring of ice in the punch bowl for a cheery brunch beginning! Then grill these tiny cheese-filled burgers and your barbecue is under way.

1 quart grape juice
1 46-ounce can pineapple-grapefruit
  juice
1 quart ginger ale
Molded ice rings or ice cubes with
  cherries

Combine grape juice and pineapple-grapefruit juice in a large punch bowl (or pitcher). Add ginger ale just before serving. Make one large ice ring by filling a gelatin ring mold with water and cherries, or make individual cherry cubes in your ice cube tray if you are using a pitcher.
MAKES 14–16 SERVINGS.

CHEESE BURGERETTES

4 ounces blue cheese
1 pound ground beef
¼ cup sour cream
¼ teaspoon dill
¼ teaspoon pepper
¼ teaspoon salt

Crumble blue cheese in a bowl. Set aside. Combine ground beef, sour cream, dill, and seasonings. Form into small burgerettes, about a tablespoon each. Make an indentation in the center of each and fill with blue cheese. Broil 5–7 minutes. Serve at once.
MAKES ABOUT 24.

EGGS AND RICE SUPREME

Arrange these individual casseroles in the kitchen and heat them on the outdoor grill just before serving. Aluminum foil pans would be worthy of your consideration—neat to heat, and disposable, too!

4 cups hot cooked rice
8 hard-cooked eggs
2 tablespoons butter
1 teaspoon Worcestershire sauce
½ teaspoon salt
⅛ teaspoon pepper
4 tablespoons butter
4 tablespoons flour
2 cups milk
1 teaspoon prepared mustard
2 cups grated Swiss cheese

Divide rice into 8 individual casseroles. Cut eggs in half lengthwise; remove yolks and blend with 2 tablespoons butter, Worcestershire sauce, salt, and pepper. Stuff mixture back into cavities in egg whites; arrange 2 halves on rice in each casserole. Melt 4 tablespoons butter and blend in flour; add milk gradually, stirring constantly until thickened. Stir in mustard; then spoon over eggs. Sprinkle with cheese. Broil until topping is bubbly and lightly browned.
MAKES 8 SERVINGS.

BEAN BAGS

There's a new fashion in bean bags these days. They're made of foil and tossed right on the outdoor grill. It's your turn to catch on to an easy barbecue trick!

2 10-ounce packages frozen French-cut
   green beans
¼ cup butter
2 tablespoons minced onion
½ cup prepared marinara sauce

Place frozen beans on 2 large, double-thick squares of aluminum foil. Mash together butter, minced onion, and marinara sauce; spoon mixture over the frozen beans. Wrap foil tightly so there will be no leakage. Place on a hot grill for 20–30 minutes.

MAKES 8 SERVINGS.

FROZEN LEMON PIE

Everybody will enjoy this chocolate crumb crusted Frozen Lemon Pie. It's a no-bake delicacy that will wait politely in the freezer until serving time.

Chocolate Crumb Crust

1¼ cups finely crushed chocolate
   cookies
¼ cup melted butter
1 tablespoon sugar

Combine cookie crumbs, melted butter, and sugar; reserve ¼ cup of the mixture for garnish. Press remaining mixture against bottom and sides of a 9-inch pie plate. Chill until filling is ready.

Lemon Filling

3 eggs, separated
½ cup sugar
⅓ cup lemon juice
2 tablespoons sugar
1 cup heavy cream, whipped
1 teaspoon grated lemon rind

Beat egg yolks until very thick and light; gradually beat in ½ cup sugar and lemon juice. Beat egg whites to soft peak stage; add 2 tablespoons sugar gradually, continuing to beat at high speed until whites are stiff but not dry. Gently fold egg whites and whipped cream into lemon mixture; stir in grated rind. Spoon into prepared Chocolate Crumb Crust; sprinkle with reserved crumbs. Freeze until firm.

MAKES 8 SERVINGS.

Corned Beef 'n' Egg Bake.

APRÈS SKI BRUNCH

Remove the skis and settle down for a few hours of warmth and relaxation while you tell the tales of slalom! Start with chilled cider and hot fondue, proceed with an easy-but-delicious corned beef and egg dish, and finish with thick slices of a Walnut-Cheddar Bread that you baked ahead of time. Hearty fare for those who have braved the snowy hills!

MENU

On arrival:
CIDER
OLD ENGLISH CHEESE FONDUE*

At the table:
CORNED BEEF 'N' EGG BAKE*

For dessert:
FRESH FRUIT BOWL
WALNUT-CHEDDAR BREAD*
COFFEE

* Recipe follows

OLD ENGLISH CHEESE FONDUE

Pour out mugs of cider and pass out the fondue forks. Then watch the agile skiers jump into the action! Dunking hunks of crusty bread into creamy fondue may turn out to be the best exercise of the day.

3 cups milk
2 teaspoons Worcestershire sauce
1 teaspoon salt
½ teaspoon curry powder
¼ teaspoon pepper
¼ teaspoon onion salt
3 tablespoons flour
3 tablespoons butter
1 pound processed Old English cheese, shredded
2 loaves French or Italian bread

Measure ½ cup of the milk into a pint jar. Add Worcestershire sauce, salt, curry, pepper, onion salt, and flour. Cover tightly. Shake until all ingredients are blended. Add to fondue pot or saucepan with remaining milk and the butter. Cook and stir until thickened. Add cheese; stir until smooth. Heat bread until crisp. Break or cut into bite-size pieces. Serve with long forks to spear bread and dip into hot cheese mixture. MAKES 8–12 SERVINGS.

CORNED BEEF 'N' EGG BAKE

Here's a stick-to-the-ribs brunch dish that will win words of praise. It's a smooth run every time!

8 slices toast, cubed
6 tablespoons butter, melted
4 teaspoons instant minced onion
⅔ cup grated Cheddar cheese
2 4½-ounce cans corned beef spread
1 cup milk
½ teaspoon salt
¼ teaspoon pepper
8 eggs

Cover bottom of a large greased shallow baking dish (or small roasting pan) with toast cubes. Drizzle with melted butter. Sprinkle with onion and cheese, cover with corned beef spread. Combine milk, salt, and pepper; pour over top. Make eight hollows for the eggs. Break an egg carefully into each depression. Cover baking dish and bake at 350° for 25–30 minutes, depending on desired doneness of eggs.
MAKES 8 SERVINGS.

WALNUT-CHEDDAR BREAD

Cheddar cheese and walnuts meet in a wonderful dessert bread along with tangy seasonings. Make it the day before and slide through brunch with rare form!

2½ cups sifted all-purpose flour
2 tablespoons granulated sugar
2 teaspoons baking powder
1¼ teaspoons salt
½ teaspoon dry mustard
½ teaspoon baking soda
Dash cayenne
¼ cup shortening
1 cup grated Cheddar cheese
1 egg
1 cup buttermilk
½ teaspoon Worcestershire sauce
1 cup chopped walnuts

Resift flour with sugar, baking powder, salt, mustard, baking soda, and cayenne. Cut in shortening. Add cheese, and mix in with a fork. Beat egg lightly; add buttermilk and Worcestershire sauce. Stir into dry mixture just until moistened. Add walnuts and mix well. Turn the stiff dough into a greased 8½-inch-by-4½-inch loaf pan and smooth top. Bake in a 350° oven for 55 minutes. Let stand 10 minutes, then turn out and cool on wire rack.

MAKES 1 LOAF.

AROUND=THE=WORLD BRUNCHES

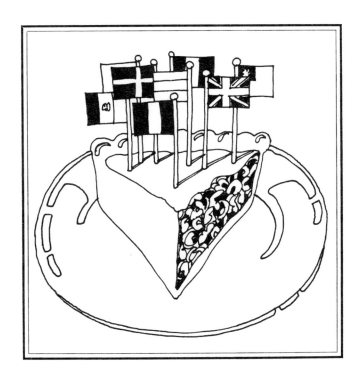

Canadian Pork Pie.

CANADIAN BRUNCH

Reflections of heritage are shown in the selected dishes below—with a few modern ingredients to make the preparations easier for you. Perhaps you can't travel north, but your table can!

MENU

On arrival:
RASPBERRY DRINK*
JOHNNY CAKE*

At the table:
YELLOW PEA SOUP*
CANADIAN PORK PIE*
GREEN SALAD

For dessert:
APPLESAUCE-NUT BREAD*
COFFEE

* Recipe follows

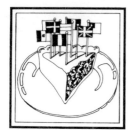

RASPBERRY DRINK

Canadian country wives make their own raspberry vinegar as a base for a popular refreshment. But you can use a bottled syrup and get much the same effect.

1 quart bottled raspberry syrup, undiluted
3 quarts ice cold water or carbonated water

Mix the drinks individually as ordered, using 2 tablespoons syrup (or follow directions on the bottle) to a glass of cold water or carbonated beverage.·
MAKES SIXTEEN 8-OUNCE DRINKS.

JOHNNY CAKE

Serve a traditional Johnny Cake in a new way—as an appetizer for brunch. Canadian ancestors used maple sugar, but here brown sugar is used as a tasty substitute. Serve it with softened butter and a bowl of maple syrup for those who are not watching their waists.

½ cup brown sugar
1 egg
1 cup sour cream
1 cup cornmeal
1 cup flour
1 teaspoon baking soda
½ teaspoon salt
Maple syrup (optional)
Softened butter (optional)

Combine brown sugar and the egg; stir in sour cream. Mix together the cornmeal, flour, baking soda, and salt. Add this mixture to the egg mixture, beating until smooth. Pour this batter into a greased 1-quart pan. Bake at 350° until browned. Cut in wedges and serve with softened butter and maple syrup (for dunking) if desired.
MAKES 8 SERVINGS.

YELLOW PEA SOUP

Yellow Pea Soup is a heritage from old Quebec, and well worth its survival. Here it is followed by a slice of Canadian Pork Pie designed to take advantage of modern products. Different and delicious!

1 pound dried yellow peas
½ pound salt pork, cut in small cubes
3 onions, minced
2 quarts water
1 teaspoon salt
½ teaspoon pepper

Soak dried peas overnight; drain. Put them in a large kettle, add cubes of salt pork and minced onion. Add water, salt, and pepper. Simmer for 2–3 hours. Skim the surface of the soup as needed to remove pea skins and scum. Cook until peas are very soft. For smooth soup, put it through a food mill before serving.
MAKES 8 SERVINGS.

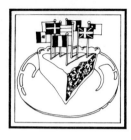

CANADIAN PORK PIE (*TORTIÈRE*)

2 pounds lean ground raw pork
½ cup cranberry-orange relish
1 teaspoon salt
½ teaspoon pepper
¼ teaspoon nutmeg
1 onion, chopped
2 tablespoons cornstarch
1 cup chicken broth
1 package pie crust mix
1 egg, beaten (optional)

Combine raw pork with cranberry-orange relish, salt, pepper, and nutmeg. Add chopped onion, and cornstarch stirred into chicken broth. Simmer mixture for 30 minutes, stirring occasionally to prevent sticking. Cool. Prepare pie crust according to package directions. Roll out ½ of crust and use it to line bottom and sides of an 8-inch pie pan. Pour filling into pie pan. Roll out top crust and cover pie; seal edges with water; slash crust to allow steam to escape. Brush pie with beaten egg, if desired. Bake in 375° oven for 35–40 minutes, or until crust is golden brown.
MAKES 4 SERVINGS.

APPLESAUCE-NUT BREAD

Apples and nuts are plentiful in Canada and are used in many recipes. Here you find them together in an intriguing Applesauce-Nut Bread—served for dessert.

2 cups sifted flour
1 teaspoon baking soda
½ teaspoon baking powder
½ teaspoon cinnamon
½ teaspoon salt
½ cup salad oil
1 cup sugar
2 eggs, beaten
1 cup applesauce
3 tablespoons apple juice
½ teaspoon vanilla
1 cup chopped walnuts

Preheat oven to 350°. Grease and flour an 8-inch square pan. Sift flour, baking soda, baking powder, cinnamon, and salt together. Thoroughly combine oil and sugar; add eggs and applesauce and beat well. Add sifted dry ingredients. Add apple juice and vanilla. Mix well; add nuts. Pour batter into prepared pan, bake for 1 hour at 350°, until well-browned and slightly shrunk from sides of pan. Cool. Cut into 2-inch squares.

MAKES 8 SERVINGS.

Sweet and Sour Chicken and Chinese Almond Cookies.

CHINESE BRUNCH

Just for a change of pace, plan to serve a Chinese-style brunch! Here are some cook-at-home dishes combined with an appetizer from your freezer. Have a bottle of soy sauce available for those who want extra flavoring. Accompany all with a large pot of tea throughout the meal, if you wish.

MENU

On arrival:

PINEAPPLE JUICE

FROZEN EGG ROLLS

At the table:

SHRIMP SINGAPORE*

SWEET AND SOUR CHICKEN*

BOILED RICE

CHINESE FRIED NOODLES

For dessert:

KUMQUATS

LICHEE NUTS

CHINESE ALMOND COOKIES*

TEA

* Recipe follows

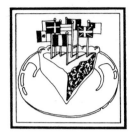

SHRIMP SINGAPORE

Shrimp and bananas are the base of this famous Far Eastern dish, Shrimp Singapore. You'll find it is an exotic delicacy.

2 pounds shrimp, cooked, shelled, and deveined
¼ cup butter
¼ cup flour
1 teaspoon curry powder
1 teaspoon salt
⅛ teaspoon cayenne
2 chicken bouillon cubes
2 cups boiling water
4 bananas

Be sure that shrimp has been cooked for only 2–3 minutes in boiling water. Melt butter in a skillet; remove from heat and stir in flour, curry powder, salt, and cayenne. Dissolve bouillon cubes in boiling water; gradually add this to flour mixture, stirring until smooth. Return to heat and cook, stirring constantly, until sauce is smooth and thickened. Peel bananas, cut in half crosswise; then in thirds lengthwise. Add to sauce. Cover pan and cook slowly, stirring frequently, about 5 minutes, or until bananas are tender. Add shrimp and cook just long enough to heat shrimp through.
MAKES 8 SERVINGS.

SWEET AND SOUR CHICKEN

*If you haven't got a Chinese wok avail-
able, a large skillet will do for this
quickly made Sweet and Sour Chicken.
Serve it with freshly boiled rice and
packaged Chinese fried noodles, available at your market. It's the kind of
recipe that you can make "chop-chop"!*

2 large whole chicken breasts
¼ cup butter
2 cups diagonally sliced celery
2 onions, thinly sliced
1 16-ounce can pineapple chunks
2 1¼-ounce envelopes chicken gravy
   mix
2 tablespoons vinegar
½ cup toasted slivered almonds

Remove raw chicken from bones; cut into bite-sized pieces.
Melt butter and lightly brown chicken pieces, celery, and onion.
Drain the juice from pineapple into a pint measuring cup; add
enough water to make 2 cups. Stir this diluted juice into the
chicken. Add pineapple chunks, chicken gravy mix, and
vinegar. Bring to a boil, stirring constantly; then cover and
simmer for 5 minutes. Serve, sprinkled with almonds, on hot
boiled rice.

MAKES 8 SERVINGS.

CHINESE ALMOND COOKIES

You'll find canned kumquats and packaged lichee nuts with the Chinese food in your market. Do serve them with these delicious almond cookies for a tasty dessert selection. Refill the teapot to go with this.

2½ cups sifted all-purpose flour
¾ cup sugar
1 teaspoon baking powder
¼ teaspoon salt
¾ cup butter
1 egg
2 tablespoons water
1½ teaspoons almond extract
30 whole blanched almonds
1 egg yolk, beaten

Sift flour with sugar, baking powder, and salt into a medium-size bowl. Using pastry blender or 2 knives, cut in butter until mixture resembles corn meal. Beat egg with water and almond extract. Add to flour mixture, mixing with a fork until dough leaves sides of bowl. On lightly floured surface, knead dough until smooth. Chill 1 hour. Make 1-inch balls of dough; place on ungreased cookie sheets and flatten each cookie to ¼ inch with palm of hand. Press almond into center of each cookie. Combine egg yolk with small amount of water; brush on cookies. Bake in 350° oven for 20 minutes, until golden brown. MAKES 2½ DOZEN COOKIES.

ENGLISH BRUNCH

For an English-inspired brunch, try this derby-and-cane menu on as many lords and ladies as you can round up. It's about as far from Carnaby Street as you can get—with a definite upper-class flavor!

MENU

On arrival:
HOT BUTTERED APPLE RUM*
STILTON CHEESE AND CRACKERS

At the table:
BROILED KIPPERS
EGGS DELLA ROBBIA*

For dessert:
TRIFLE*
TEA

* Recipe follows

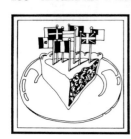

HOT BUTTERED APPLE RUM

Serve mugs of Hot Buttered Apple Rum and help-yourself cheese and crackers for a warm beginning. If you can't get to Piccadilly Circus—'ave a 'appy 'oliday anyway!

2 quarts apple juice
½ cup brown sugar
¼ cup butter
1 jigger of rum for each mug
Nutmeg

Heat apple juice and sugar until sugar is dissolved and juice reaches boiling point. Add butter. Put rum in each mug. Pour on hot apple juice mixture. Sprinkle with nutmeg.
MAKES ABOUT 16 SERVINGS.

EGGS DELLA ROBBIA

Along with a platter of broiled kippers, pass individual portions of Eggs della Robbia—the crunchy base is toasted English muffins. Cauliflower in cheese sauce crowns the circles of grilled Canadian bacon and poached eggs!

2 10-ounce cooking pouches frozen
  cauliflower in cheese sauce
8 slices Canadian bacon, grilled
4 English muffins, split and toasted
8 eggs, poached (see page 100)
Paprika

Slip frozen cooking pouches of cauliflower in cheese sauce into about 3 cups of boiling water. Bring to a second boil. Cook 16 minutes, turning several times to ensure complete cooking. Arrange grilled bacon slice on a muffin half on each serving plate; top with hot poached egg. Spoon hot cauliflower in cheese sauce over each egg; sprinkle with paprika. MAKES 8 SERVINGS.

TRIFLE

Be sure to prepare the Trifle in a large glass bowl so the lovely layers are visible while you serve. It's a perfect froth of a dessert!

1 3¼-ounce package vanilla pudding
  and pie filling
2½ cups milk
8-inch sponge cake layer
½ cup raspberry jam
1 17-ounce can sliced peaches
1 cup heavy cream, whipped
Maraschino cherries
Toasted slivered almonds

Prepare pudding mix as directed on package, increasing milk to 2½ cups. Cover with wax paper; set aside. Split sponge cake into two layers. Spread jam on one layer; top with the other. Cut cake into small squares. Drain peaches, reserving ¾ cup syrup. Quickly dunk cake squares in the reserved syrup. Put half of the squares in the serving dish; cover with ½ cup sliced peaches. Top with half of the pudding; repeat layering, ending with pudding. Decorate top of Trifle with whipped cream. Garnish with cherries and toasted slivered almonds. MAKES 8 SERVINGS.

Sausage Quiche.

FRENCH BRUNCH

If it's a French-styled brunch that intrigues you, here's one with just the flair you'll love. It's been designed with a joie de vivre *that puts the accent on easy cooking.*

MENU

On arrival:
POTAGE À LA CHAMPAGNE*
FROMAGE DU PAIN*

At the table:
SAUSAGE QUICHE*
SAVORY SHRIMP*
CURLY ENDIVE SALAD

For dessert:
CHOCOLATE-WALNUT MOUSSE*
COFFEE

* Recipe follows

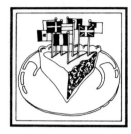

POTAGE A LA CHAMPAGNE

When your guests arrive, hand them mugs of hot pea soup that's tingling with champagne. Then pass a tray of freshly broiled cheese-bread. Irresistible!

2 10½-ounce cans condensed green pea
   soup
1 cup water
⅛ teaspoon mace
⅛ teaspoon tarragon
1 cup heavy cream
2 cups champagne

Combine condensed green pea soup, water, mace, and tarragon in the blazer pan of a chafing dish. Blend thoroughly. Place over medium heat of burner. Bring to a gentle boil. Fold in slightly beaten heavy cream and reheat. Do not allow to bubble. Add champagne and ladle at once into heated mugs. MAKES 4 SERVINGS.

FROMAGE DU PAIN

8 ounces blue cheese
1 egg, beaten
2 teaspoons Worcestershire sauce
1 loaf French bread, cut in ½-inch
   slices

Combine blue cheese with egg and Worcestershire sauce. Beat until smooth. Place bread slices on a cookie sheet and spread each slice generously with cheese mixture. Broil 3 minutes. Serve at once.
MAKES ABOUT 2 DOZEN SLICES.

SAUSAGE QUICHE

It is suggested that this Sausage Quiche be baked in a square pan to make serving easier. The broiled shrimp and simple salad round out the main course. Your taste buds will say, "C'est magnifique!"

1 package pastry mix for two-crust pie
1 pound little pork sausage links
1 egg
¼ teaspoon salt
Dash pepper
½ cup light cream
½ cup shredded Swiss cheese
1 tablespoon flour

Preheat oven to 425°. Prepare pastry according to directions on the package; roll dough out on lightly floured surface to a 10-inch square. Fit into an 8-inch square pan, folding sides to make a double rim ¾" high.

For filling: cook sausage links according to package directions. Drain and cool. Arrange links in two rows on unbaked crust. Combine egg with salt and pepper; add light cream and beat until well blended. Toss flour with cheese and stir into egg mixture. Pour this filling over sausage links. Bake 12–15 minutes, or until knife inserted in center comes out clean. Cut into squares for serving.
MAKES 6–8 SERVINGS.

SAVORY SHRIMP

2 pounds jumbo shrimp, fresh or frozen
¼ pound butter
1 tablespoon chopped scallions
1 teaspoon minced garlic
½ teaspoon salt
¼ teaspoon pepper
2 tablespoons chopped fresh parsley

If shrimp are frozen, let them thaw on paper towels to absorb moisture. Peel shrimp, but do not remove the tail shells. Slit shrimp down the center of inside curved surface. Cut each shrimp almost through to the back, but do not puncture skin on back side. Remove veins. Place butter in mixing bowl with scallions, garlic, salt, pepper, and parsley; blend all ingredients together. Place shrimp on preheated broiling pan, slit side up; place a dab of butter mixture on each shrimp. Broil 5 minutes. MAKES 6–8 SERVINGS.

CHOCOLATE-WALNUT MOUSSE

What would a French menu be without a marvelous mousse? The pièce de résistance *here is a Chocolate-Walnut Mousse that tastes like a chef's dream come true—with or without the Mocha Cream garnish!*

1 6-ounce package semisweet chocolate
morsels
½ cup milk
2 teaspoons unflavored gelatin
2 tablespoons cold water
2 eggs, separated
⅛ teaspoon salt
⅛ teaspoon cream of tartar
3 tablespoons granulated sugar
1 cup whipping cream
3 tablespoons light rum, brandy, or
orange flavored liqueur (optional)
½ cup chopped walnuts
Mocha Cream (recipe follows)

Combine chocolate and milk in top of double boiler, and heat over hot water until chocolate melts. Meanwhile soften gelatin in cold water. Beat egg yolks lightly. When chocolate has melted, stir gelatin and egg yolks into it, and cook 3–4 minutes, stirring constantly, until gelatin is melted and egg yolks cooked. Remove from heat and cool. When chocolate mixture has cooled to room temperature, beat egg whites with salt and cream of tartar until stiff. Gradually beat in sugar, continuing to beat to a stiff meringue. With same beater whip cream. Stir rum, brandy, or liqueur into chocolate mixture, then fold in meringue, whipped cream, and walnuts. Turn into a 6-cup mold, and chill for several hours or overnight. Unmold and garnish with Mocha Cream.
MAKES 8 SERVINGS.

Mocha Cream

½ cup heavy cream
1 teaspoon sugar
½ teaspoon instant coffee powder

Whip cream with sugar and instant coffee powder. Fill cake decorator and garnish mousse with rosettes.

*Meatballs Paprikash, and Broccoli
with Parsley-Cream Sauce.*

HUNGARIAN BRUNCH

You may hear your guests rhapsodize over this interesting brunch, inspired by the hearty cuisine of Hungary. If the tender dessert pancakes don't fit into your cooking schedule, buy some strudel as a fine substitute—cheese, with raisins, if possible.

MENU

On arrival:
PINEAPPLE COCKTAIL*
LECSÓ DIP*

At the table:
MEAT BALLS PAPRIKASH*
NOODLES
BROCCOLI WITH PARSLEY-CREAM SAUCE*

For dessert:
APRICOT PANCAKES*
COFFEE

Recipe follows

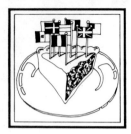

PINEAPPLE COCKTAIL

You'll think you're sipping a champagne cocktail when you splash some club soda into the pineapple-wine mixture just before serving. Lecsó is a popular dish used as an appetizer or served with an omelet. Use it here as a delicious dip.

1 1-pound can pineapple tidbits
1 tablespoon sugar
2 tablespoons lemon juice
1 bottle white wine
Ice cubes
1 pint plain carbonated soda

Combine pineapple tidbits and juice from can with sugar, lemon juice, and wine. Ladle into champagne glasses and, just before serving, add ice cubes and a splash of plain carbonated soda for a champagne effect.
MAKES 8 SERVINGS.

LECSÓ DIP

3 green peppers
3 tomatoes
1 tablespoon butter
1 onion, chopped
4 strips bacon, diced
1 teaspoon sugar
½ teaspoon salt
½ teaspoon paprika

Cut the green peppers into thin strips, removing seeds and membranes. Dip the tomatoes into boiling water for a moment, remove skins; then cut in quarters. Melt butter in a skillet, add onion and stir until onion is just translucent. Add diced bacon and cook over low heat until limp. Add strips of green pepper and quartered tomatoes. Sprinkle with sugar, salt, and paprika. Cover and simmer for 15–20 minutes, until peppers are tender and tomatoes are puréed. Place over a warmer and serve hot as a dip.

MAKES ABOUT 1½ CUPS DIP.

MEAT BALLS PAPRIKASH

Veal and sour cream join paprika in this tasty Hungarian dish of Meat Balls Paprikash. Serve it hot on broad buttered noodles.

1 pound ground beef
1 pound ground veal
1 cup bread crumbs
¾ cup milk
¼ cup minced onion
1 teaspoon salt
¼ teaspoon Tabasco sauce
¼ teaspoon chervil
¼ teaspoon tarragon
2 tablespoons flour
1 pint sour cream
½ cup milk
1 tablespoon paprika
Cooked noodles

Combine ground meats, bread crumbs, ¾ cup milk, onion, ½ teaspoon salt, Tabasco, chervil, and tarragon. Shape into balls about 1 inch in diameter. Boil in salted water 10–12 minutes. Drain. Meanwhile, prepare sauce by combining flour, remaining salt, and sour cream in a saucepan; stir until smooth. Add ½ cup milk and paprika. Heat, stirring constantly until smooth and thickened. Do not boil. Add meat balls. Serve with hot cooked broad ·noodles.

MAKES 8 SERVINGS.

BROCCOLI WITH PARSLEY-CREAM SAUCE

3 10-ounce packages frozen broccoli
    spears
2 tablespoons butter
1½ tablespoons flour
¾ cup heavy cream
1 tablespoon chopped parsley
¼ teaspoon salt
Dash of pepper

Prepare broccoli spears as directed on the package. Meanwhile melt the butter; add flour and stir together. Slowly add cream, stirring constantly until mixture is thickened. Remove from heat and add chopped parsley, salt, and pepper. Pour over drained broccoli spears and serve.
MAKES 8 SERVINGS.

APRICOT PANCAKES

These Apricot Pancakes are light as a feather due to the addition of carbonated soda water to the batter. Keep finished pancakes heated in a 200° oven while you are making the rest. No need to worry about leftovers with these—there won't be any!

2 eggs
1 cup milk
1 cup club soda
2 cups sifted flour
¼ teaspoon salt
1 teaspoon vanilla extract
¼ pound butter, melted
1 cup apricot jam
1 cup ground walnuts
Confectioner's sugar

Stir eggs, milk, and soda together quickly. Add flour and salt, stirring constantly. Add vanilla. Using an 8-inch skillet, and a pastry brush for the melted butter, spread just enough butter to grease pan. Heat. Ladle in just enough batter to cover the bottom of the skillet by tilting it from side to side. As soon as the pancake is browned on one side, brush a bit of butter in the pan as you lift the pancake to brown it on the other side. Once you have browned the pancake on both sides, spread jam over it, roll it up, and keep it warm while you make the rest. When all are made, sprinkle them with ground walnuts and confectioner's sugar. Serve warm.
MAKES ABOUT 24 PANCAKES.

Prune Chremslach.

ISRAELI BRUNCH

This Israeli-inspired brunch begins and ends with pancakes, but of a taste and variety that are superb. You don't have to be a Jewish mother to cook like one!

MENU

On arrival:
ORANGE JUICE
POTATO PANCAKES WITH
APPLESAUCE*

At the table:
HADDOCK BALLS*
CARROT TSIMMES*

For dessert:
PRUNE CREMSLACH*
COFFEE

* Recipe follows

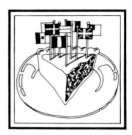

POTATO PANCAKES
WITH APPLESAUCE

*The secret of good potato pancakes is
to make them with freshly grated raw
potato and fry them in peanut oil. Make
them tiny if you are serving them as an
appetizer.*

2 pounds potatoes, pared
1 onion
1 egg, slightly beaten
2 tablespoons flour or matzoh meal
½ teaspoon salt
¼ teaspoon pepper
1 cup peanut oil
Applesauce

Grate potatoes and onions into a deep bowl. Add the beaten
egg, flour, salt, and pepper. Heat oil in a large skillet. Drop
small spoonfuls of mixture into the hot oil and fry. Turn
pancakes when brown on one side. Serve with cold applesauce.

MAKES 8 SERVINGS.

HADDOCK BALLS

*Any kind of bland fish may be used
instead of haddock in the recipe below.
The Tsimmes is a blend of sweet and
sour fruits mixed with carrots to create
an unforgettable taste. "Tsimmes"
means fuss—so make one, your guests
will love it!*

½ cup finely chopped onion
3 tablespoons butter
3 tablespoons flour
½ cup milk
2 teaspoons salt
¼ teaspoon pepper
1 teaspoon dry mustard
1 pound haddock, cooked and flaked
2 cups cooked rice
2 teaspoons lemon juice
2 tablespoons water
1 egg, slightly beaten
Fine bread crumbs

Cook onion in butter until soft but not brown. Blend in flour;
add milk, salt, pepper, and mustard. Add haddock, rice, and
lemon juice. Chill. Form into balls. Mix water and egg; dip
haddock balls into egg mixture. Roll in crumbs. Chill several
hours. Fry in deep fat (375°) 3–4 minutes, until browned.
MAKES 8 SERVINGS.

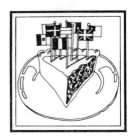

CARROT TSIMMES

2 10-ounce cooking pouches frozen carrot nuggets in butter sauce
4 thin orange slices, cut in half
4 thin lemon slices, cut in half
1 8¾-ounce can pineapple tidbits, drained
2 tablespoons pineapple syrup
¼ cup firmly packed brown sugar
2 teaspoons cornstarch
¼ cup chopped walnuts

Slip pouches of carrots into boiling water. Bring water to a second boil; continue cooking 18 minutes. Open pouches and drain butter sauce into small bowl. Combine carrot nuggets with orange and lemon slices and pineapple in 1½-quart casserole. Stir pineapple syrup, brown sugar, and cornstarch into butter sauce; mix well. Pour over carrots. Sprinkle with walnuts. Bake at 350° for 20–30 minutes.

MAKES 6–8 SERVINGS.

PRUNE CHREMSLACH

A chremsel is usually served at Passover meals, but it is really too good to reserve just for that holiday. It has a filling of prunes, and a Prune-Almond Sauce topping. The plural spelling is chremslach. You'll be serving many of them!

Batter

6 large eggs
1 cup warm water
3 tablespoons melted shortening
2 teaspoons salt
1½ tablespoons sugar
¼ teaspoon cinnamon
3¼ cups matzoh meal

Beat eggs; add water and melted shortening. Beat in salt, sugar, cinnamon, and matzoh meal. Chill until firm enough to shape (1–2 hours). Roll half of dough on a board or surface sprinkled with matzoh meal, to ⅛-inch thickness. Cut into 24 three-inch circles. Place 1 rounded tablespoon prune filling in center of each. Roll out remaining dough. Cut into 24 three-inch circles. Place atop filling and seal edges. Pan fry in oil until golden on both sides.

MAKES 2 DOZEN FILLED PRUNE CHREMSLACH.

Filling

2 1-pound jars cooked prunes
¼ cup chopped walnuts
¼ cup pineapple or apricot preserves
1 tablespoon lemon juice

While dough is chilling, drain prunes, reserve liquid. Pit and chop. Combine with walnuts, preserves, and lemon juice.

MAKES 1¾ CUPS FILLING.

Prune-Almond Sauce

½ cup sugar
2 teaspoons potato starch
½ teaspoon cinnamon
1 cup cold prune juice
2 tablespoons lemon juice
2 tablespoons blanched, slivered almonds

Mix together sugar, starch, and cinnamon. Gradually blend in prune juice and lemon juice. Heat, stirring constantly, until mixture is thickened and clear. Add almonds. Serve hot or cold with Prune Chremslach.

MAKES ABOUT 1 CUP SAUCE.

Deviled Pizza Loaf.

ITALIAN BRUNCH

When in Rome—follow the local dining customs. But when at home, an Italian-inspired brunch can be a romantic departure from the usual ham 'n' eggs. Try it and see!

MENU

On arrival:
CHILLED SPUMANTI
DEVILED PIZZA LOAF*

At the table:
ITALIAN ANTIPASTO*
FETTUCINI ALFREDO*
ITALIAN BREAD STICKS

For dessert:
NEAPOLITAN ICE CREAM PIE*
ESPRESSO

* Recipe follows

DEVILED PIZZA LOAF

Start with chilled spumanti—a sparkling wine of good repute. For the non-drinkers present, chilled grape juice would be a suitable substitute. Both will be enhanced by a wedge of Deviled Pizza Loaf below!

2 4½-ounce cans deviled ham
¼ cup tomato sauce with tomato bits
½ teaspoon dried crushed oregano
2 8-ounce cans refrigerated crescent
    dinner rolls
2 tablespoons grated Parmesan cheese
1 tablespoon melted butter

Combine deviled ham, tomato sauce, and oregano. Unroll crescent roll dough; separate into 8 rectangles. Pat each rectangle to flatten and close diagonal serrated lines. Cut each in half, parallel to short edge, to make 16 rectangles. Spread 8 with a level tablespoon of deviled ham mixture not quite to edges. Roll up each starting from long edge. Arrange rolls in single layer (seam side down) in lightly greased 9-inch-by-5-inch loaf pan parallel with long side of pan. Sprinkle with 1 tablespoon Parmesan cheese. Spread remaining rectangles with a rounded tablespoon of deviled ham mixture, proceed as above to form second layer in loaf pan. Brush top lightly with butter, sprinkle with remaining cheese. Bake at 375° for 40 minutes, or until top is deep brown and center of loaf is done. Remove from pan to cool slightly. Serve warm.

MAKES 8 SERVINGS.

ITALIAN ANTIPASTO

Arrange a large platter of antipasto and let your guests pass it around for a selection of tangy delicacies. Then serve the famous Fettucini Alfredo—so simple to prepare and yet a beautiful offering. Sesame seeded bread sticks make it even more authentic for all!

8 thin slices Italian salami
8 thin slices prosciutto
8 small wedges melon, peeled
1 2-ounce can anchovies
2 7-ounce cans tuna fish
1 6-ounce jar artichoke hearts in oil
1 can whole pimientos
2 large green peppers, cut in wedges
 and seeded
8 thick tomato slices
8 large green olives
8 large black olives

Arrange all ingredients attractively on a large platter. Wrap prosciutto around slices of melon before placing on platter. MAKES 8 SERVINGS.

FETTUCINI ALFREDO

2 pounds fettucini
8 quarts water
1 tablespoon salt
½ pound butter, softened
1 cup grated Parmesan cheese

Cook fettucini in boiling salted water for 7–10 minutes, until tender. Drain thoroughly and transfer to a heated serving bowl. Add half the butter and toss; add half the cheese and toss. Repeat and mix well. Serve at once. MAKES 8 SERVINGS.

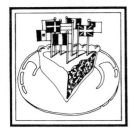

NEAPOLITAN ICE CREAM PIE

Famous for ice cream the world over, Italians especially like multiflavor combinations. Here's an ice cream pie that offers a trio of tastes in a chocolate cookie crust!

1 cup chocolate wafer crumbs
3 tablespoons sugar
¼ cup butter, melted
1 pint chocolate ice cream, softened
1 pint strawberry ice cream, softened
1 pint vanilla ice cream, softened
½ cup shredded toasted coconut

Combine chocolate crumbs with sugar in a 10-inch pie plate. Add melted butter and mix well with a fork. Press mixture firmly with back of a metal spoon over bottom and sides of pie pan. Chill for 15 minutes. Place the chocolate ice cream in bottom of wafer crust, spread strawberry ice cream over chocolate, and top with vanilla ice cream. Sprinkle top with toasted coconut. Freeze until firm.

MAKES 8 SERVINGS.

MEXICAN BRUNCH

You don't have to travel south of the border for a Mexican brunch. It can happen in your own kitchen. Here is a menu that uses foods readily available at your local market and turns them into Mexican delights!

MENU

On arrival:
FRUIT PUNCH*
GUACAMOLE*

At the table:
HUEVOS RANCHEROS AMERICANO*
SHRIMP SARAPICO*
TORTILLA BISCUITS*

For dessert:
FRUIT AMBROSIA*
MEXICAN HOT CHOCOLATE*

* Recipe follows

FRUIT PUNCH

Start with a glass of chilled Fruit Punch accompanied by a popular Guacamole dip. Do use corn chip crackers to keep the mood authentic!

3 cups orange juice
4 12-ounce cans guava nectar
1 cup freshly cut orange cubes
1 cup freshly cut pineapple cubes
Mint sprigs
Ice cubes

Combine orange juice and guava nectar. Add cubed fruit. Garnish cups of punch with mint sprigs. Add ice cubes before serving.
MAKES 8–12 SERVINGS.

GUACAMOLE

2 large ripe avocados
3 tablespoons lime juice
1 tomato, peeled
2 tablespoons grated onion
1 clove garlic, mashed or pressed
½ teaspoon salt
3 drops Tabasco sauce

Peel avocados and cut in half to remove seeds. Mash pulp with lime juice to keep it from darkening. Add tomato and mash to a smooth consistency. Add grated onion and mashed garlic. Add salt and Tabasco. Chill until ready to serve.
MAKES ABOUT 2 CUPS OF DIP.

HUEVOS RANCHEROS AMERICANO

Follow the individual servings of baked eggs with individual aluminum foil packets of Shrimp Sarapico. Serve both with refrigerator-born Tortilla Biscuits. An almuerzo *with style!*

¼ cup chopped onion
2 tablespoons chopped green pepper
1 large clove garlic, minced
1 teaspoon chili powder
2 tablespoons butter
1 10¾-ounce can condensed tomato soup
⅓ cup water
¼ cup sliced ripe olives
Dash Tabasco sauce
8 eggs
Salt and pepper
Shredded Cheddar cheese

In a saucepan, cook onion, green pepper, garlic, and chili powder in butter until vegetables are tender. Stir in soup, water, olives, and Tabasco sauce. Heat; stir now and then. Spoon 3 tablespoons of soup mixture into each of 8 individual shallow baking dishes; break an egg in each. Salt and pepper to taste. Bake at 350° for 12–15 minutes, or until eggs are set. Sprinkle cheese over eggs. MAKES 8 SERVINGS.

SHRIMP SARAPICO

1 pound cream cheese
1 pound Roquefort cheese
8 pimientos, chopped
4 dozen shrimp, cleaned and peeled
2 lemons, sliced thin
1 cup white wine

Make a paste of the cream cheese, Roquefort cheese, and chopped pimientos. Divide the paste among 8 squares of aluminum foil, each about 12–14 inches square. Place 6 cleaned shrimp on each nest of paste, and top with 2 thin slices of lemon on each. Close the aluminum bag by pinching the top together. However, just before you seal the bag, pour an ounce of white wine into it. Place the bags on a cookie sheet and bake at 350° for 20–30 minutes. Serve each guest a foil packet to be opened at the table.

MAKES 8 SERVINGS.

TORTILLA BISCUITS

2 8- or 9½-ounce packages refrigerated
   flaky biscuits
1½ cups corn meal

Stretch and flatten biscuits to 4-inch rounds. Dip in corn meal, coating both sides well. Place on greased cookie sheets and bake at 350° for 12–15 minutes, or until lightly browned.
MAKES 8–12 SERVINGS.

FRUIT AMBROSIA

Fruit and coconut are frequent ingredients in Mexican cookery. Here they are combined into a satisfying dessert. Your sweet tooth will be further pleased with the cinnamon-flavored hot chocolate, and if you have a molinillo *(chocolate beater), now is the time to use it.*

2 16-ounce cans peach halves
2 bananas, sliced
3 tablespoons lemon juice
1 cup shredded coconut

Empty peaches with juice into a large glass compote. Sprinkle banana slices with lemon juice and arrange on top of peach halves. Sprinkle coconut over all.
MAKES 8 SERVINGS.

MEXICAN HOT CHOCOLATE

4 ounces unsweetened chocolate
¼ cup sugar
2 teaspoons cinnamon
2 quarts milk

Combine the ingredients in the top of a double boiler saucepan. Cook over hot water until chocolate is melted; then beat until foamy.
MAKES 8 SERVINGS.

Salad Romanoff.

RUSSIAN BRUNCH

Although brunch is not a favored time for entertaining in Russia, the cuisine is readily adapted to it. This menu presents some favorite dishes in ways that will suit any party.

MENU

On arrival:
UNCLE VANYA COCKTAIL*
ZAKUSKA*

At the table:
CAVIAR OMELET*
SALAD ROMANOFF*
BLACK BREAD

For dessert:
RUSSIAN APPLE PIE*
TEA

* Recipe follows

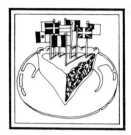

UNCLE VANYA COCKTAIL

In Russia you should be able to take your vodka straight and swift; but in case you can't, here's a cocktail that lets you sip it slowly. With it is a Za-kuska—an array of unadorned appetizers to whet your tastebuds.

2 ounces blackberry brandy
1 ounce vodka
1 tablespoon lemon juice
Twist of lemon peel

Shake brandy, vodka, and lemon juice together. Pour over ice and add a twist of lemon peel.
MAKES 1 SERVING.

ZAKUSKA

You may choose any number of simply presented dishes as an appetizer. The entire offering is called a Zakuska. Many of the items are available at your local delicacy shop, or in jars at your market. Here is a suggested variety:

Platter of sliced sturgeon and smoked salmon.
Bowl of liver paté.
Bowl of pickled mushrooms.
Bowl of shrimp in mayonnaise.
Bowl of sliced fresh cucumbers in sour cream.
Platter of sliced Swiss cheese.
Tray of thinly sliced black bread.

CAVIAR OMELET

Normally a Zakuska would include some kind of caviar, but for this menu the caviar has been reserved for the omelet.

16 eggs
¼ cup red caviar
¼ cup milk
½ teaspoon salt
⅛ teaspoon pepper
3 tablespoons butter

Break eggs into a large bowl. Beat with a fork until yolks and whites are combined. Add caviar, milk, salt, and pepper; stir with care not to break the caviar. Divide the butter between two large skillets; heat until butter is melted. Pour batter into both skillets; when undersides are done, turn heat low and cover pans until top sides are solidified. Slide omelets onto heated platters and serve.
MAKES 8 SERVINGS.

SALAD ROMANOFF

This herring and beet salad is another combination of foods that are particularly loved in Russia!

Lettuce cups
2 1-pound cans julienne beets, chilled and drained
2 6-ounce jars herring in wine sauce
1 onion, sliced and separated into rings
1 8-ounce bottle creamy Russian dressing

Continued on next page

SALAD ROMANOFF/Continued

Line salad bowl with lettuce cups. Arrange beets around edge and fill center with herring. Garnish with onion rings. Serve with Russian dressing.

MAKES 8 SERVINGS.

RUSSIAN APPLE PIE

This apple pie is bursting with fruit and nuts in a combination you will want to eat again and again! Do serve it with tea—from a samovar if you're lucky enough to have one.

8 to 10 large apples
¾ cup raisins
¾ cup sugar
1 tablespoon freshly grated orange rind
¼ cup finely chopped almonds
2 tablespoons butter
2 tablespoons cherry jam
Pastry for a 2-crust 10-inch pie

Peel and core apples; slice thin. Add raisins, sugar, grated orange rind, and chopped almonds. Mix all together. Spoon half the mixture into the bottom crust of the pie; dot with half the butter and cherry jam. Spoon the rest of the apple mixture into crust and top with dots of remaining butter and jam. Top with pastry and prick or slash top crust to allow steam to escape. Bake in a 350° oven for 45–55 minutes, until pie is nicely browned.

MAKES 8 SERVINGS.

SCANDINAVIAN BRUNCH

What's the next best thing to traveling to Scandinavia? Tasting some of their wonderful food! Here's a sampling for all voyagers who have an invitation to your dining room.

MENU

On arrival:
SWEDISH GLOGG*
HERRING TIDBITS

At the table:
DANISH CHEESE PUFF*
SLICED HAM
DILLED CUCUMBERS*
SWEDISH CRISPBREAD

For dessert:
PRUNE CRESCENTS*
COFFEE

* Recipe follows

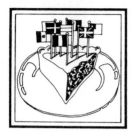

SWEDISH GLOGG

Although Swedish Glogg is traditionally served at Christmas time, it is just too good to miss at other times of the year, too. Serve it with a platter of several different kinds of herring cut into bite-sized pieces for easy handling.

1 bottle burgundy
1 bottle vodka or aquavit
10 crushed cardamon seeds
5 whole cloves
dried rind of 1 orange
1½-inch cinnamon stick
¼ cup sugar
1 cup blanched almonds
1 cup raisins

In a saucepan, combine burgundy and vodka. Tie crushed cardamon seeds, cloves, orange rind, and cinnamon stick into a cheesecloth bag. Put this in the saucepan of wine mixture. Add sugar, almonds, and raisins. Bring mixture to a simmering point well below boiling and stir well. (Boiling will evaporate the alcohol so be careful only to heat it.) After several minutes, remove bag of seasonings. Place glogg on a warmer and ladle into small cups when ready to serve. Be sure to provide spoons for the raisins and nuts that sink to the bottom of each cup.

MAKES 8–12 SERVINGS.

DANISH CHEESE PUFF

Denmark is a country of remarkable dairy products, so what could be more representative than this Danish-style cheese puff. It is a mellow blend of bread cubes, flavorful cheese, and a simple custard of eggs and milk poured over. Serve it with thick slices of baked ham, and pass the Dilled Cucumbers for a zinging farm brunch!

2 cups diced samsoe cheese
8 slices white bread, cut in small cubes
6 eggs
3 cups milk
½ teaspoon salt
⅛ teaspoon pepper
⅛ teaspoon nutmeg

Butter a 1½-quart casserole, and alternate layers of cubed bread and cheese, beginning and ending with bread. Beat eggs with milk, salt, pepper, and nutmeg. Pour over contents of casserole, covering bread completely. Bake in preheated 350° oven for 45–50 minutes, until casserole is set and top is golden brown and puffed.
MAKES 6–8 SERVINGS.

DILLED CUCUMBERS

2 large cucumbers
1 large onion, sliced paper thin
1 large sprig fresh dill, cut up
1 cup wine vinegar
½ cup water
2 tablespoons salad oil
2 teaspoons sugar
1 teaspoon salt
½ teaspoon pepper

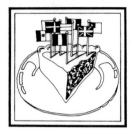

DILLED CUCUMBERS/Continued

Peel cucumbers and run the tines of a fork lengthwise down each to give it serrated edges when sliced. Slice paper thin. Place in a small deep bowl alternating with layers of onion and dill. Combine vinegar, water, salad oil, sugar, salt, and pepper. Pour over cucumbers and refrigerate, covered, for several hours or overnight.

MAKES 8 SERVINGS.

PRUNE CRESCENTS

If you can't get to Tivoli Gardens for a taste of Danish pastry, make your own from your market's dairy case. These are made from crescent roll dough. They are a tempting blend of fruit, spice, and yeasty nuttiness that makes your efforts worthwhile.

1 15-ounce jar cooked prunes
¼ cup ground almonds
½ teaspoon cinnamon
1 package refrigerator crescent rolls

Drain prunes, use the juice for a drink another time. Pit prunes and mash or puree in blender. Mix with almonds and cinnamon. Separate crescent roll dough into 8 triangles. Divide the filling among the triangles, placing in the center of triangle. Roll up, forming a crescent. Bake in a 400° oven 8–10 minutes, until browned.

MAKES 8 CRESCENTS.

SPANISH BRUNCH

No time for involved cooking, but still want to serve a Spanish-style brunch? The answer is here in a multitude of quick tricks from your local market, which leave you time for a Flamencó or two!

MENU

On arrival:
SANGRÍA COCKTAIL*
TAPAS*

At the table:
GAZPACHO*
PANTRY PAELLA*

For dessert:
FRESONES*
COFFEE

* Recipe follows

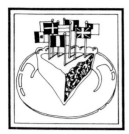

SANGRÍA COCKTAIL

Start with Sangría and fruit on the rocks for a tingling welcome to your guests. Tapas are small bowls of spicy foods for casual nibbling before the meal— just enough to whet the appetites!

1 bottle Sangría
1 lemon, cut in thin slices
1 orange, cut in thin slices
Ice cubes

Pour Sangría into a pitcher. Add slices of fruit and let stand until ready to serve. Put ice cubes in each glass and pour Sangría over them, making sure that some fruit is included. MAKES 8 COCKTAIL SERVINGS.

TAPAS

Place several small bowls filled with the following items, readily available at your market in cans or jars:

Whole mushrooms: Drain and sprinkle with garlic powder and dried parsley. Toss and serve.
Black olives: Drain and sprinkle with grated onion and a pinch of oregano.
Pickled beets: Drain and serve.
Three bean salad: Drain and serve.
Pimientos: Drain and sprinkle with garlic powder.
Garlic-flavored croutons

GAZPACHO

Serve chilled Gazpacho in small bowls for a taste of Madrid—but make it in your blender the easy way. Follow with a star of Spanish cookery, a paella that combines rice, saffron, seafood, poultry, and vegetables. It is named after the pan in which it is served.

2 10½-ounce cans condensed cream of
    tomato soup
¼ cup wine vinegar
2 cloves garlic, minced
2 cups water
¼ cup olive oil
1 cucumber, cut up
1 onion, cut up
1 green pepper, cut up
2 teaspoons sugar
1 teaspoon salt
½ teaspoon pepper
2 hard-cooked eggs, chopped

Place all ingredients, except chopped eggs, in your blender with as much of the 2 cups of water as it will hold. Blend well. Empty into a bowl and stir in remaining water until smooth. Chill. Serve cold with chopped eggs as a garnish.
MAKES 8 SERVINGS.

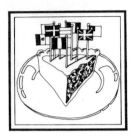

PANTRY PAELLA

8 chicken thighs
1 tablespoon melted butter
1½ cups clam juice
2 8-ounce cans minced clams
½ teaspoon saffron
2 cups long grain rice, uncooked
2 4½-ounce cans deveined jumbo shrimp, drained and rinsed in water
1 8-ounce can large whole oysters, drained
1 1-pound can tiny peas, heated and drained
1 pimiento, cut in strips
¼ cup black olives

Brush chicken thighs with melted butter and broil under medium heat for 7 minutes on each side. Meanwhile pour clam juice, including that drained from canned clams, into a 2-cup measure; add water if necessary to bring to a 2-cup level. Pour into saucepan or paella pan. Add 1½ cups more water and bring liquid to a boil. Add saffron and rice. Cook for 15 minutes. Place broiled chicken, clams, shrimp, and oysters on top of rice and continue cooking until rice is light and fluffy and seafood is heated through. Sprinkle peas over all and garnish with strips of pimiento and olives.
MAKES 6–8 SERVINGS.

FRESONES

Fresones are fresh plump strawberries. Here they are showered with orange juice and topped with sweetened whipped cream. There'll be a stampede to this rich red dessert. Olé!

1 quart plump fresh strawberries
Juice of 1 fresh orange
1 pint heavy cream, whipped
1 tablespoon confectioner's sugar

Hull and wash strawberries. Chill. Pour orange juice over berries just before serving and top with a generous amount of whipped cream. Sprinkle confectioner's sugar over all. MAKES 8 SERVINGS.

Bishop's Bread and Almond Mocha.

VIENNESE BRUNCH

Here's a Viennese-inspired brunch menu that will tickle the taste buds with nostalgia. It starts with a delectable cold soup and ends with a choice of two desserts—and perhaps a waltz!

MENU

On arrival:
KALTSCHALE*

At the table:
HAM AND KRAUT CASSEROLE*
AUSTRIAN WAX BEANS*

For dessert:
BISHOP'S BREAD*
PRUNE BAVARIAN*
ALMOND MOCHA*

* Recipe follows

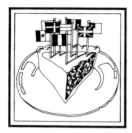

KALTSCHALE

Kaltschale is an icy cold fruit soup with an addition of dry wine for extra refreshment. Add another tablespoon of tapioca and serve it as a chilled dessert another day!

1 17-ounce can peeled apricots
1 17-ounce can Elberta peach halves
1 tablespoon quick tapioca
1 cup dry white wine

Pit apricots. Place apricots and peaches, with syrup, in electric blender and blend until thick soup stage is reached. Pour into saucepan and add tapioca. Cook until tapioca becomes transparent. Remove from stove and chill in refrigerator. Mix wine into fruit mixture just before serving. Pour into stemmed fruit glasses.
MAKES ABOUT 8 SERVINGS ½ CUP EACH.

HAM AND KRAUT CASSEROLE

Apples and sauerkraut make a tasty bed for cubes of cooked ham in this casserole below. Serve it with zesty wax beans reminiscent of the Blue Danube country!

2 cups cooked ham, cut in ½-inch pieces
6 cups sauerkraut
½ cup diced onion
3 tablespoons lemon juice
1 tablespoon caraway seeds
3 medium apples, sliced and cored

In a large bowl, mix the ham, sauerkraut, diced onion, lemon juice, and caraway seeds. Place a layer of the kraut mixture on the bottom of a large greased casserole. Cover with a layer of sliced unpeeled apples. Alternate layers until casserole is filled; finish with a top layer of sliced apples. Cover and bake in a 350° oven for 30 minutes. MAKES 8–10 SERVINGS.

AUSTRIAN WAX BEANS

8 slices bacon, diced
1 cup sliced green onions
2 16-ounce cans diagonal-cut wax beans, drained
½ cup white wine vinegar
¼ cup sugar
¼ cup diced pimiento

Fry bacon in a skillet until crisp. Drain, reserving about 3 tablespoons bacon drippings in skillet. Add onions to skillet; sauté for 2 minutes. Add beans, vinegar, sugar, and pimiento; heat thoroughly. MAKES 8 SERVINGS.

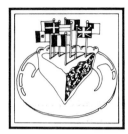

BISHOP'S BREAD

When is a bread not a bread? When it's a cake! This Bishop's Bread is chock full of chocolate morsels, almonds, and glazed cherries. It bakes up sweet and light.

3 cups prepared biscuit mix
¾ cup sugar
1 egg
1¼ cups orange juice
¼ cup slivered blanched almonds
¼ cup glazed cherries, halved
¼ cup white seedless raisins
1 6-ounce package semisweet chocolate
    morsels
Confectioner's sugar (optional)

Combine biscuit mix and sugar in a bowl. Add egg and orange juice; beat hard for 30 seconds. Stir in almonds, cherries, raisins, and chocolate morsels. Turn into a greased and floured 9-inch-by-5-inch loaf pan or 2-quart mold. Bake in a 350° oven for 55–60 minutes. Cool before slicing. Sprinkle with confectioner's sugar, if desired.

MAKES 8–10 SERVINGS.

PRUNE BAVARIAN

Rich Prune Bavarian looks like you spent hours preparing it, but it takes only minutes and is quite delectable.

1 1-pound 9-ounce jar cooked prunes
1 envelope unflavored gelatin
½ cup sugar
2 tablespoons lemon juice
½ teaspoon vanilla extract
1½ cups heavy cream, lightly whipped

Drain syrup from prunes; sprinkle syrup with gelatin and let stand 5 minutes. Stir over low heat until gelatin is dissolved. Stir in sugar. Cool until syrupy; stir in lemon juice and vanilla extract. Cool until mixture mounds on spoon. Fold in whipped cream. Pit prunes, arrange around bottom edge of a 1½-quart dessert mold. Reserve a dozen prunes for garnish. Spoon cream mixture into mold. Chill for several hours, until set. To serve, unmold on a chilled platter, garnish with reserved prunes and more whipped cream, if desired. MAKES 8 SERVINGS.

ALMOND MOCHA

Instead of serving coffee, serve the traditional Viennese beverage, Almond Mocha, made in moments with modern ingredients. It's like taking a stroll down the Kaerntnerstrasse!

3 heaping teaspoons quick chocolate-flavored mix
1 level teaspoon instant coffee

Combine ingredients in a cup. Fill cup with hot milk. Top with unsweetened whipped cream, flavored with almond extract. MAKES 1 SERVING.

INDEX

A

ALMOND MOCHA, 199
ANNIVERSARY BRUNCH, 81–86
ANTIPASTO, ITALIAN, 173
APPLE(S)
Noggin, Hot Spiced, 34
Pie, Russian, 184
Polisher's Cocktail, 114
Rum, Hot Buttered, 150
Waldorf Salad Mold with, 36
APPLESAUCE
Cupcakes, Butterfly, 32
Doughnuts, 112
Nut Bread, 143
Potato Pancakes with, 166
Soufflé, 79
APRÈS SKI BRUNCH, 131–34
APRICOT
Cooler, 30
Pancakes, 162–63
AROUND THE WORLD BRUNCHES, 137–99
ARTICHOKES, AND CREAMED HAM, 46

ASPARAGUS WITH PIMIENTO STRIPS, 48
ASPIC
Cranberry Vegetable Mold, 42
Sauterne, 116
AUSTRIAN WAX BEANS, 197
AVOCADO
Dill Sauce, 122
Guacamole, 176

B

BABY SHOWER BRUNCH, 71–76
BACON
Canadian
Eggs Della Robbia with, 150
Glazed Roast, 22
Cheese Nut Loaf with, 6
-Chicken Liver Rolls, 92
-Oyster Chowder, 40–41
BANANA COCONUT BITES, 62
BARBECUE BRUNCH, 125–30
BEAN(S)
Austrian Wax, 197
Bags, 128

BEEF
  Corned
    Egg Bake with, 133
    Walnut Glazed, 17
  Dried, with Pickles, 110
  Fondue with Mushrooms,
    120–22
  Ground
    Cheese Burgerettes, 126
    Football Hamburgers, 110–
      11
  Meat Balls Paprikash, 161
BEFORE THE GAME BRUNCH,
  109–12
BEVERAGES
  Almond Mocha, 199
  Apricot Cooler, 30
  Chocolate, Mexican Hot, 179
  Citrus Fizz, 98
  Cocktails
    Apple Polisher's, 114
    Bloody Mary, 26
    Pineapple, 160
    Pink Lady, 62
    Sangria, 190
    Uncle Vanya, 182
  Cranberry Whirl, 40
  Eggnog, 46
  Fruit Float, 117
  Glogg, Swedish, 186
  Irish Coffee, 19
  Noggin, Hot Spiced Apple, 34
  Punch
    Cranberry Cheer, 4
    Fruit, 176
    Limeade, 13
    Lullaby, 72
    Purple, 126
    Royal Peach Champagne,
      82
    Tutti-Frutti, 56
    Valentine, 10
  Raspberry Drink, 140
  Rum, Hot Buttered Apple, 150
  Wine
    Champagne Flip, 68
    Mulled, 78
    Sangria Cocktail, 190
    Swedish Glogg, 186
BIRTHDAY BRUNCH, 55–60
BISCUITS
  Toasted, 64
  Tortilla, 178
BISHOP'S BREAD, 198
BLOODY MARY, 26
BLUE CHEESE SAUCE, 122
BLUE CHEESE TURNOVERS, 114
BON VOYAGE BRUNCH, 87–90
BOUILLON, HOT CLAM AND
  TOMATO, 88
BRANDIED HARD SAUCE, 50
BREAD AND ROLLS
  Applesauce Nut Bread, 143
  Blue Cheese Turnovers, 114
  Cheese 'n' Bacon Nut Loaf, 6
  Cinnamon Raisin Bread, 101
  Cornbread-Sausage Puff, 31
  Deviled Pizza Loaf, 172
  Devilish Danish, 34
  Doughnuts, Applesauce, 112
  Fromage du Pain, 154
  Johnny Cake, 140
  Prune Crescents, 188
  Sesame Triangles, 74
  Soda Bread, Sweet Irish, 18
  Suprise Corn Muffins, 84
  Toasted Biscuits, 64
  Tortilla Biscuits, 178
  Walnut Cheddar Bread, 134
BRIDAL SHOWER BRUNCH, 61–66
BRIDGE BRUNCH, 103–8
BROCCOLI
  Omlet with Mushroom Sauce,
    93
  with Parsley-Cream Sauce,
    162
BUTTERFLY APPLESAUCE CUP-
  CAKES, 32

C

CABBAGE-LIME GELATINE MOLD,
18
CAKE
Applesauce Cupcakes,
Butterfly, 32
Bishop's Bread, 198
Chicken 'n' Ham "Birthday
Cake," 57–58
Macaroon Coffee Cake,
94–95
Mocha Walnut Torte, 65
CANADIAN BRUNCH, 139–44
CANADIAN PORK PIE, 142
CARROT TSIMMES, 168
CAVIAR
Dip, 10
Omelet, 183
CHAMPAGNE
Flip, 68
Royal Peach Punch, 82
CHEDDAR BUNNIES, 22
CHEESE
American
Macaroni Casserole, 58
Salami Firecrackers, 26
Sherried Mold, 72
Bacon Nut Loaf, 6
Blue
Burgerettes with, 126
Fromage du Pain, 154
Sauce, 122
Sherried Mold, 72
Turnovers, 114
Burgerettes, 126
Cheddar
Bacon Nut Loaf with, 6
Bunnies, 22
Football Hamburgers, 110–
11
Mushroom Soufflé with,
11–12
Sauce, 99–100

Sherried Crackers with,
104
Walnut Bread with, 134
Cream
"Birthday Cake" Frosting,
57–58
Pimiento Rounds with, 68
Red Caviar Dip with, 10
Scrambled Eggs with, 4
Sherried Mold, 72
Fondue, 120, 132
Gruyère, Fondue with, 120
Old English, Fondue, 132
Samsoe, Danish Puff with,
187
Stilton, Crackers and, 149
Swiss, Egg Supreme with, 127
CHERRY JUBILEE SAUCE, 13
CHICKEN
'n' Ham "Birthday Cake," 57–
58
Livers
Bacon Rolls with, 92
Kabobs, 83
Saucy, 30
Paella, Pantry, 192
Salad Mold, 63
Shortcake, 70
Supreme, 74
Sweet and Sour, 147
Chinese Almond Cookies, 148
CHINESE BRUNCH, 145–48
CHOCOLATE
Cloud Pie, 106–7
Crumb Crust, 128
Fondue, 123
Mexican Hot, 179
Walnut Mousse, 156–57
CHOWDER, BACON-OYSTER, 40–41
CHREMSLACH, PRUNE, 168
CHRISTMAS DAY BRUNCH, 48–50
CINNAMON-RAISIN BREAD, 101
CITRUS FIZZ, 98
CLAM(S)

CLAM(S) *continued*
  and Tomato Bouillon, 88
  Paella, Pantry, 192
COCKTAIL FRANKS WITH APRICOT
  DIP, 56
COCKTAILS, *see* BEVERAGES
COCONUT
  Banana Bites with, 62
  Sherry Cream Pie, 24
  Fruit Ambrosia, 179
  Peach Sunbursts, 59
COFFEE, IRISH, 19
COOKIES, CHINESE ALMOND, 148
CORN
  Fritters with Sausages, 27
  Muffins, Surprise, 84–85
CORNBREAD-SAUSAGE PUFF, 31
CORNED BEEF
  'n' Egg Bake, 133
  Walnut-Glazed, 17
CRAB QUICHE, 79
CRACKERS, SHERRIED CHEESE,
  104
CRANBERRY
  Cheer Punch, 4
  Vegetable Aspic Mold, 42
  Whirl, 40
CREAMED HAM AND ARTICHOKE
  HEARTS, 46
CREAMY FUDGE SAUCE, 28
CUCUMBERS, DILLED, 188
CURRIED DIP, 110

D

DANISH CHEESE PUFF, 187
DANISH PASTRY
  Devilish, 34
  Prune Crescents, 188
DATE AND NUT BREAD, 90
DEVILED PIZZA LOAF, 172
DEVILED SCRAMBLED EGGS, 115
DEVILISH DANISH, 34
DILLED CUCUMBERS, 188

DIP
  Apricot, 56
  Curried, 110
  Fish 'n', 16
  Lescó, 160
  Red Caviar, 10
DOUGHNUTS, APPLESAUCE, 112

E

EASTER SUNDAY BRUNCH, 21–24
EGG(S)
  Benedict, 105
  Broccoli Omlet with Mush-
    room Sauce, 93
  Corned Beef Bake, 133
  Della Robbia, 150–51
  Deviled, 89
  Rancheros Americano, 177
  in Rice Ring with Cheddar
    Sauce, 99–100
  and Rice Supreme, 127
  Scrambled
    with Cream Cheese, 4
    Deviled, 115
    Mushroom-Chive, 82–83
    Puffy, 73
EGGNOG, 46
ENGAGEMENT BRUNCH, 119–24
ENGLISH BRUNCH, 149–52

F

FETTUCINI ALFREDO, 173
FISH
  n' Dip, 16
  See also Haddock; Salmon;
    Tuna
FONDUE
  Beef and Mushrooms, 120–22
  Chocolate, 123
  Cheese, 120
    Old English, 132
FOURTH OF JULY BRUNCH, 25–
  28

FRANKFURTERS, COCKTAIL, WITH APRICOT DIP, 56
FRENCH BRUNCH, 153–58
FRESONES, 193
FRITTERS, CORN, WITH SAUSAGES, 27
FROMAGE DU PAIN, 154
FROZEN LEMON PIE, 128–29
FRUIT
  Ambrosia, 179
  Float, 117
  Kaltschale, 196
  Orange Baskets, 78
  Punch, 176
  Salad Mold, 47–48
  Snowball Pudding with, 49
  Stuffed Prunes, 98–99
  Tutti-Frutti Punch, 32
  See also specific fruits

G

GAZPACHO, 191
GLAZED BACON ROAST, 22
GLAZED BRUNCH LOAF, 115
GLOGG, SWEDISH, 186
GRADUATION BRUNCH, 113–18
GRILLED SAUSAGES, 4
GUACAMOLE, 176
GUEST OF HONOR BRUNCH, 97–102

H

HADDOCK
  Balls, 167
  Fish 'n' Dip, 16
HALLOWEEN BRUNCH, 33–38
HAM
  "Birthday Cake" with Chicken and, 57–58
  Creamed, and Artichoke Hearts, 46
  Deviled Pizza Loaf, 172
  Devilish Danish, 34
  Kraut Casserole with, 196
  Layered Glazed, 94
  Mousse, 69
  Potato Pancakes Stuffed with, 5–6
  with Waffles and Fruit Sauce, 41
HARVEST SHRIMP CASSEROLE, 35
HOLIDAY BRUNCHES, 3–50
HOLLANDAISE SAUCE, 105
HONEY CRUNCH SUNDAE PIE, 27–28
HOT BUTTERED APPLE RUM, 150
HOT CLAM AND TOMATO BOUILLON, 88
HOT CORN FRITTERS AND SAUSAGES, 27
HOT SPICED APPLE NOGGIN, 34
HOUSEWARMING BRUNCH, 77–80
HUEVOS RANCHEROS AMERICANO, 177
HUNGARIAN BRUNCH, 159–64

I

ICE CREAM
  Fruit Float, 117
  Peach Sunbursts, 59
  Pie, Neapolitan, 174
IRISH COFFEE, 19
IRISH POTATOES, 17
ISRAELI BRUNCH, 165–70
ITALIAN ANTIPASTO, 173
ITALIAN BRUNCH, 171–74

K

KALTSCHALE, 196

L

LABOR DAY BRUNCH, 29–32
LEMON PIE, FROZEN, 129
LESCÓ DIP, 160

LIMEADE PUNCH, 16
LIME-CABBAGE GELATINE MOLD, 18
LIVERS, CHICKEN
Bacon Rolls with, 92
Kabobs, 83–84
Saucy, 30
LOBSTER, OPEN-HEARTED SALAD, 11
LULLABY PUNCH, 72

M

MACARONI AND CHEESE CASSEROLE, 58
MACAROON COFFEE CAKE, 94–95
MEAT BALLS PAPRIKASH, 161
MERINGUE, PEACH SUNBURSTS WITH, 59
MEXICAN BRUNCH, 175–80
MEXICAN HOT CHOCOLATE, 179
MOCHA
Almond, 199
Cream, 157
Walnut Torte, 65
MOLASSES PECAN PIE, 43
MOUSSE
Chocolate-Walnut, 156–57
Ham, 69
MUFFINS, SURPRISE CORN, 84–85
MULLED WINE, 78
MUSHROOM(S)
and Beef Fondue, 120–21
-Cheese Soufflé, 11–12
Sauce, with Broccoli Omelet, 93
Scrambled eggs with chives and, 82

N

NEAPOLITAN ICE CREAM, 174
NEW YEAR'S DAY BRUNCH, 3–8

O

OLD ENGLISH CHEESE FONDUE, 132
OMLET, see EGGS
OPEN-HEARTED LOBSTER SALAD, 11
ORANGE
Baskets, 78
Ginger Sauce, 121
Pie, 75
ORANGE-GLAZED TURKEY ROLL, 42
OYSTER(S)
Bacon-Chowder, 40–41
Paella, 192

P

PAELLA, PANTRY, 192
PANCAKES
Apricot, 162–63
Potato
with Applesauce, 166
Stuffed, 5–6
PANTRY PAELLA, 192
PARSLEY-CREAM SAUCE, 162
PASTRIES
Devilish Danish, 34
Prune Crescents, 188
See also Bread and Rolls
PEA SOUP
à la Champagne, 154
Yellow, 141
PEACH(ES)
Royal Champagne Punch, 82
Spiced, 63
Sunbursts, 59
PECANS, DATE BREAD WITH, 90
PICKLES
in a Blanket, 110
Curried Dip for, 110
PIE
Apple, Russian, 184
Chocolate Cloud, 106–7

Honey Crunch Sundae, 27–28
Ice Cream, Neapolitan, 174
Lemon, Frozen, 129
Molasses Pecan, 43
Pork, Canadian, 142
Orange, 74
Sherry Coconut Cream, 24
Sherry-Pumpkin Chiffon, 37
PIMIENTO
-Cheese Rounds, 68
Strips, with Asparagus, 48
PINEAPPLE COCKTAIL, 160
PINK LADY COCKTAIL, 62
POACHED SALMON STEAKS, 100
PORK PIE, CANADIAN, 142
POTAGE À LA CHAMPAGNE, 154
POTATO(ES)
Irish, 17
Pancakes
with Applesauce, 166
Stuffed, 5–6
POTS DE CRÈME, 85
PRUNE(S)
Bavarian, 199
Chremslach, 168–69
Crescents, 188
Stuffed, 98–99
PUDDING, STEAMED SNOWBALL, 49
PUFFY SCRAMBLED EGGS, 73
PUMPKIN-SHERRY CHIFFON PIE, 37
PUNCH, see BEVERAGES
PURPLE PUNCH, 126

Q

QUICHE
Crab, 79
Sausage, 155

R

RAISIN BREAD, CINNAMON, 101
RASPBERRY DRINK, 140

RED CAVIAR DIP, 10
RICE
Bavarian, 12–13
Ring, 36
Ring with Eggs, 99–100
and Eggs Supreme, 127
ROLLS, see BREAD AND ROLLS
ROYAL PEACH CHAMPAGNE PUNCH, 82
RUM, HOT BUTTERED APPLE, 150
RUSSIAN APPLE PIE, 184
RUSSIAN BRUNCH, 181–84

S

ST. PATRICK'S DAY BRUNCH, 15–20
ST. VALENTINE'S DAY BRUNCH, 9–14
SALAD
Antipasto, Italian, 173
Chicken Mold, 63
Cranberry-Vegetable Aspic Mold, 42
Fruit Mold, 47–48
Guacamole, 176
Lime-Cabbage Gelatine Mold, 18
Lobster, Open-Hearted, 11
Romanoff, 183
Shrimp, Seagoing, 88–89
Waldorf Whip Mold, 36
SALAMI FIRECRACKERS, 26
SALMON
Poached Steaks, 100
Zakuska, 182
SANGRIA COCKTAIL, 190
SAUCE
Avocado Dill, 122
Brandied Hard, 50
Cheddar, 99
Cherry Jubilee, 13
Creamy Fudge, 28
Fruit, 41

Hollandaise, 105
Lemon Topping, 23
Mushroom, 93
Orange-Ginger, 21
Orange Topping, 21
Parsley-Cream, 162
Prune-Almond, 169
SAUCY CHICKEN LIVERS, 30
SAUERKRAUT
and Ham Casserole, 196–97
-Raisin Bake, 111
SAUSAGE
Corn Fritters with, 27
-Cornbread Puff, 31
Grilled, 5
Quiche, 155
SAUTERNE ASPIC, 116
SAVORY SHRIMP, 156
SCANDINAVIAN BRUNCH, 185–88
SEAFOOD
Paella with, 192
See also specific seafood
SESAME TRIANGLES, 74
SHERRIED CHEESE CRACKERS,
104
SHERRIED CHEESE MOLD, 72
SHERRY COCONUT CREAM PIE, 24
SHERRY-PUMPKIN CHIFFON PIE,
37
SHRIMP
Harvest Casserole, 35
Paella, 192
Sarapico, 178
Savory, 156
Seagoing Salad, 88–89
Singapore, 146
Soup, Frosty, 104
Tureen, 84
SNOWBALL PUDDING, STEAMED,
49
SOUFFLÉ
Applesauce, 80
Mushroom-Cheese, 11–12
SOUP

Bacon-Oyster Chowder, 40–41
Frosty Shrimp, 104
Gazpacho, 191
Hot Clam and Tomato
Bouillon, 88
Pea
à la Champagne, 154
Yellow, 141
SPANISH BRUNCH, 189–94
SPECIAL OCCASION BRUNCHES,
55–134
SPICED PEACHES, 63
SPICY WAFFLES, 23
STRAWBERRIES, SPANISH, 193
STUFFED POTATO PANCAKES, 5–6
STUFFED PRUNES, 98
STUFFED TOMATOES, 106
SURPRISE CORN MUFFINS, 84–85
SWEDISH GLOGG, 186
SWEET IRISH SODA BREAD, 18
SWEET AND SOUR CHICKEN, 147

TAPAS, 190
THANKSGIVING DAY BRUNCH, 39–
47
TOASTED BISCUITS, 64
TOMATO(ES)
and Clam Bouillon, 88
Stuffed, 106
TORTIÈRE, 142
TORTILLA BISCUITS, 178
TRIFLE, 151
TSIMMES, CARROT, 168
TUNA
and Noodle Stroganoff, 64
Teasers, 48
TURKEY, ORANGE-GLAZED ROLL,
42

VALENTINE PUNCH, 10
VEAL

Meat Balls Paprikash, 161
VIENNESE BRUNCH, 195–99

WAFFLES
  with Ham and Fruit Sauce, 41
  Spicy, 23
WALNUT(S)
  Applesauce Nut Bread, 143
  Cheddar Bread, 134
  Cheese-Bacon Loaf, 6
  Chocolate Mousse, 156–57
  Date Bread, 90

Glaze, for Corned Beef, 17
Mocha Torte, 65
Waldorf Salad Mold, 36
WEDDING BRUNCH, 67–70
WELCOME HOME BRUNCH, 91–96
WINE, see BEVERAGES

YELLOW PEA SOUP, 141

ZAKUSKA, 182